CONQUER YOUR SPEECHFRIGHT

LEARN HOW TO OVERCOME THE NERVOUSNESS OF PUBLIC SPEAKING

CONQUER YOUR SPEECHFRIGHT

LEARN HOW TO OVERCOME THE NERVOUSNESS OF PUBLIC SPEAKING

Karen Kangas Dwyer

Harcourt Brace College Publishers

Fort Worth Philadelphia San Diego New York Orlando Austin San Antonio

Toronto Montreal London Sydney Tokyo

Publisher	Earl McPeek
Acquisitions Editor	Carol Wada
Product Manager	Julie McBurney
Developmental Editor	Eric Carlson
Project Editor	Tamara Neff Vardy
Production Manager	Serena B. Manning
Art Director	Don Fujimoto

ISBN: 0-15-508177-2
Library of Congress Catalog Card Number: 97-74863

Copyright © 1998 by Harcourt Brace & Company

All rights reserved. No part of this publication may be reproduced or transmitted in any form or by any means, electronic or mechanical, including photocopy, recording, or any information storage and retrieval system, without permission in writing from the publisher.

Although for mechanical reasons all pages of this publication are perforated, only those pages imprinted with Harcourt Brace & Company are intended for removal.

Requests for permission to make copies of any part of the work should be mailed to: Permissions Department, Harcourt Brace & Company, 6277 Sea Harbor Drive, Orlando, Florida 32887-6777.

Address orders to:
Harcourt Brace & Company
6277 Sea Harbor Drive
Orlando, FL 32887-6777
1-800-782-4479

Address editorial correspondence to:
Harcourt Brace College Publishers
301 Commerce Street, Suite 3700
Fort Worth, TX 76102

Web site address:
http://www.hbcollege.com

Harcourt Brace may provide complimentary instructional aids and supplements or supplement packages to those adopters qualified under our adoption policy. Please contact your sales representative for more information. If as an adopter or potential user you receive supplements you do not need, please return them to your sales representative or send them to: Attn: Returns Department, Troy Warehouse, 465 South Lincoln Drive, Troy, MO 63379.

Printed in the United States of America

7 8 9 0 1 2 3 4 5 6 066 9 8 7 6 5 4 3 2 1

PREFACE

Conquer Your Speechfright is written especially for college students and anyone else who wants to overcome the fear and anxiety of public speaking. For eleven years, I have researched communication anxiety, taught university students how to overcome their excessive nervousness about speaking in public, and developed "Speaking Confidently" workshops and classes. This textbook is the result of those efforts.

This book is unique in that it presents a combination of the research-based techniques for overcoming speechfright in a user-friendly program. Several years of communication research will attest to the workable success of the combinational approach to overcoming speechfright presented here. In addition, countless numbers of my students can testify that this multidimensional program has given them (and will give you) a new confidence to speak in public situations and a changed life as a result of loosening the albatross of speechfright.

This book is written to complement a public speaking textbook **or** to be the primary textbook for a class or workshop developed specifically to help people overcome speechfright and communication anxiety. It is designed to help students reduce their speechfright and excessive nervousness about public communication so they are free to learn and polish public speaking skills. It is **not** meant to replace a public speaking textbook, as it does **not** cover public speaking skills in detail. If in fact you are reading this book on your own, as soon as you are finished, you should try to enroll in a public speaking course or other communication class where you can learn and practice public speaking skills. The confidence in public speaking that you are seeking will be acquired by using the speechfright-reduction techniques presented here in concert with practicing public speaking skills under the instruction of a communication teacher or coach.

The contents of this book are divided into three parts and twelve chapters. Part 1, "Understanding Speechfright," focuses on helping you understand your speechfright including the definition, possible causes, and impact it has on your life. Chapter One, "Speechfright and You," points out that speechfright is a common fear, and it takes commitment to conquer it. You will assess your commitment to overcoming it and write a pledge to yourself summarizing your willingness to practice the anxiety-reduction techniques.

Chapter Two, "Definitions and Assessments," discusses communication apprehension, one of the academic terms for speech anxiety. It explains the four types of communication apprehension and guides you in assessing your level and type of communication anxiety.

Chapter Three, "Causes of Speechfright," outlines several causes of communication anxiety in order to help you gain understanding about your experience. You will assess the cause(s) of your speechfright. However, you will also learn that it does not matter how or when you acquired your fear of public communication. The techniques presented in this text will help you overcome it.

Harcourt Brace & Company

Chapter Four, "Excessive Activation and the Fight or Flight Response," explains the fight or flight response, the source of your aggravating physical sensations associated with the nervousness of public speaking. You will assess your symptoms of excessive activation and learn how to stop the fight or flight response that triggers the sensations.

Part 2, "Treating Speechfright," presents an overview of the multidimensional approach to alleviating speechfright, as well as how to apply each of the speechfright-reduction techniques. Chapter Five, "Overview of Approaches and Techniques," explains the techniques and treatments in the combinational and multidimensional program, based on the acronym "BASIC ID." It stresses the importance of learning several techniques and then pinpointing the source of your speechfright as the place to begin treatment.

Chapter Six, "Deep Breathing," presents deep breathing exercises in order to induce relaxation and reduce stress. The three-minute, deep abdominal breathing exercise provides a quick-fix that brings on relaxation and is an essential part of other speechfright-reduction techniques. It targets the affect and sensation personality dimensions. You will evaluate your own breathing and then practice deep breathing exercises.

Chapter Seven, "Cognitive Restructuring," explains the four steps in this rational technique to disengage your irrational, fearful beliefs about public speaking. It targets your cognitive personality dimension. You will make a list of your fears about public speaking, identify the irrational fears and distortions, create a new list of positive coping statements, and then practice, using your coping statements to replace your old, fearful beliefs.

Chapter Eight, "Systematic Desensitization," presents the three steps in this technique that help alleviate a learned fear response to speaking in public. This technique targets the affect, sensation, and imagery personality dimensions. You will develop a hierarchy about feared events in public speaking, learn progressive muscle relaxation, and then condition relaxation in association with the events on your hierarchy.

Chapter Nine, "Mental Rehearsal (Visualization)," teaches you how to rehearse a successful speech in your mind before you present it. It targets the cognitive and imagery personality dimensions and thus helps reduce anxiety by preparing your mind for a positive communication experience. You will practice mental rehearsal to prepare for a speech just as many athletes do to prepare for a sporting event.

Chapter Ten, "Physical Exercise, Interpersonal Support, and Skills Training," discusses the importance of incorporating regular exercise, supportive friends, and public speaking skills training into your personal plan to reduce speechfright. Physical exercise targets the drugs/biological personality dimension and helps reduce tension in general, as well as public speaking anxiety. Social support from friends targets the interpersonal relationships personality dimension, by helping buffer the impact of stress, and helping you stay committed to the important goal of conquering speechfright. Public speaking skills training targets the behavior personality dimension and helps build confidence and competence in public speaking. In this chapter, you will learn a warm-up exercise and complete a public speaking skills checklist.

Part 3, "Developing a Personal Plan for Conquering Speechfright," explains how to pinpoint the personality dimension where your speechfright originates and then how to match techniques to your personality dimensions in order to create a personal action plan. Chapter Eleven, "A Multidimensional Approach," summarizes the personality dimensions effected by speechfright using BASIC ID. You will determine the firing order of your personality dimensions involved in speechfright as well the root of your anxiety. Then you will learn to match techniques to your personality dimensions.

Chapter Twelve, "An Action Plan," summarizes the plan you will follow to conquer your speechfright. You need to commit yourself to the goal of conquering speechfright, actively learn the techniques, practice the techniques, and participate in public communication in order to develop and use your skills. You will develop a practice schedule for your action plan.

SUPPLEMENTAL MATERIALS

In addition to the text, a 100-minute *"Conquering Speechfright"* audio tape is available to help you learn and practice the speechfright-reduction techniques. The tape was specifically developed for college students who are enrolled in or are about to enroll in a public speaking, basic communication, or business and professional speaking course.

The tape explains the state-of-the-art, research-proven techniques for overcoming speechfright. The techniques are described in detail so you can learn them by diligent practice with the tape, during a time that is most convenient for you. The speechfright alleviation techniques on the tape include cognitive restructuring, systematic desensitization (with deep muscle relaxation), mental rehearsal (also called visualization), deep abdominal breathing and physical exercises. The situations targeted on the tape involve those encountered when delivering a graded speech to a classroom of students.

An Instructor's Manual, written by the author, is also available for instructors. The manual includes unit and course outlines, lesson plans, exercises, assignments, and suggested readings.

ACKNOWLEDGMENTS

I owe special gratitude to my husband Larry for his loving support and editorial advice. I also want to thank a special group of friends for their continued support throughout this project: Arlene Christofferson, Cheryl Wild, Dee Golda, Willyne Dickey, Suella Stalder, Diane White, Gwen Schuman, Jetta Skinner, Pat Stover, Brenda Chauvin Scott, Chris Phillips, Mary Kay Selden, Rachel Cortese, Kate Brennan, Martie Jaworski, and Michaeleen Boulay. In addition, I am grateful for the encouragement from my forever friend Michelle Tilts and my parents Lyle and Fern Miller.

I would like to thank the following reviewers for their comments:

Vincent Bloom, California State University, Fresno
E. Sam Cox, Central Missouri State University
Cynthia Finch, Pennsylvania State University
Tim Hopf, Washington State University
Joanna Pucel, St. Cloud State University
David Waddle, Miami-Dade Community College, Wolfson

I am also grateful to Steven Booth-Butterfield, West Virginia University, for his advice and instruction that helped me immensely in developing my first special section of a public speaking course for students experiencing excessive fear of public communication.

Lastly, I would like to thank all the students who have attended my "Speaking Confidently" and public speaking classes over the years, especially Allen and Linda Minnig,

Kim Brett, Karma Camphor, Rebecca Ruetsch, Brett Franksmann, Ken Estee, Suzanne Kirk, Ed Hibberd, Yvette Osby, Joni Dick, and Irina Gotcu Mulvey I dedicate this book to them.

Karen Kangas Dwyer, Ph.D.
Public Speaking Fundamentals Course Coordinator/Director
Department of Communication
University of Nebraska at Omaha, 1998

CONTENTS

Part 2 TREATING SPEECHFRIGHT 37

Part 1

Understanding Speechfright

CHAPTER ONE

Speechfright and You

CHAPTER TWO

Definitions and Assessments

CHAPTER THREE

Causes of Speechfright

CHAPTER FOUR

Excessive Activation and the Fight or Flight Response

CHAPTER ONE

SPEECHFRIGHT AND YOU

Congratulations! You have just made one of the best decisions of your life. You have *decided* to take action to conquer your speechfright. *Deciding* to take action is the first step in overcoming a fear or anxiety about public speaking. The next step is to acquire the necessary skills and tools to help you reach that goal. This handbook will give you those tools and set you in the right direction to achieve your goal. **YOU CAN CONQUER SPEECHFRIGHT.**

1.1 A COMMON FEAR

You may think you are alone in your fear of public speaking. The truth is YOU HAVE A LOT OF COMPANY. In fact, recent surveys involving thousands of college students and adults indicate that between 70 to 75 percent of our population reports a fear of public speaking (McCroskey, 1993; Richmond & McCroskey, 1995). In other words, almost three out of every four people around you would say they are anxious or nervous when it comes to giving a speech.

❄ ❄ ❄

Christy, age 18, said: " I thought I was the only one who ever dreaded giving a speech. In fact, I thought my fear, nervousness, and trembling at the thought of giving a speech was a problem that no one else had ever experienced. . . . What a relief to know that many people have had this same fear and have been able to conquer it."

❄ ❄ ❄

The Book of Lists ranks the fear of public speaking as the number one "common fear" in America, even above the fear of dying (Wallechinsky, Wallace, and Wallace, 1977). In fact, when Americans were asked to rank their greatest fears, 41 percent listed the fear of giving a speech, while only 19 percent listed the fear of death (Bruskin Report, 1973). Consequently, if you thought you were alone in your fear about public speaking, now you know that a majority of those around you experience a similar anxiety. However, you are different from this majority. You have made a decision to take the important steps to conquer your fear.

Harcourt Brace & Company

1.2 A GOOD FIRST STEP

In the past, you may have hoped your fear and excessive nervousness about public speaking would miraculously disappear. When it didn't, you may have felt your speechfright was hopeless and you should simply try to avoid public speaking. However, you soon discovered you couldn't avoid public communication and still accomplish your personal goals. Consequently, you acquired this book in an effort to help you conquer the problem.

Actively reading this handbook, completing the exercises, and practicing the techniques **WILL HELP YOU.** No matter how long you have had a fear of public speaking, no matter how intense your nervousness has become, and no matter where your public speaking anxiety originated, YOU CAN OVERCOME IT. The techniques presented in this book are supported by more than fifty years of communication research involving numerous communication scholars, educators, and counselors. They have helped thousands of students and adults of all ages manage their anxiety and nervousness about public speaking. So be assured you have taken the first step toward conquering your fear.

❋ ❋ ❋

Trevor, age 21, had tried everything he could to avoid speaking in public. He said: "I've even offered to write a 25-page paper in lieu of giving a speech for a class assignment. . . . Although I was able to avoid public speaking in high school, in college it became increasingly difficult to avoid it. It was starting to affect my grades. . . . Finally, I decided to conquer this fear. . . . It's one of the best things I've ever done. The speechfright-reduction techniques really work."

❋ ❋ ❋

1.3 THE KEYS TO SUCCESS

Learning to overcome speechfright is like learning a new sport or new language. There are important keys to success including:

1. commitment,
2. active learning,
3. practice, and
4. participation.

For example, consider an athletic sport that you enjoy and have learned to do well. At first, you probably watched the game and made a *commitment* to learn as much as you could about the sport. You probably employed *active learning* by reading books and magazine articles about the game. At the same time, you became actively involved in learning the sport with other players, as well as with a coach who could guide you in improving your skills. Then you made a commitment to *practice.* You probably planned a practice schedule. Then you practiced a lot. Finally, you *participated* in the game at every opportunity so you could use your new skills and become an even better player.

Using the same keys that helped you learn a new sport or language, you can learn to overcome your fear of public speaking. You will need to make a *commitment* to work (put

Exercise 1.3 Your Commitment

Before you read any further, please get a pencil and write out answers to the following questions:

1. Have you ever accomplished something in your life that took a lot of time and practice?

   Was your accomplishment worth your effort?

2. Are you willing to diligently practice the techniques necessary to conquer your speechfright, since practicing the techniques is essential to reducing your fear?

3. How much time and effort are you willing to spend to overcome your speechfright (e.g., one hour per day, three hours per week)?

4. Based on your answers to these three questions, please write a pledge to yourself that summarizes your commitment to conquering speechfright and your willingness to practice the techniques presented in this handbook. Then **sign and date this contract** with yourself.

DATE ____ TIME ___ SIGNATURE ______________________________

Now, **tear out this page and post it** *in a place where you can see it often to remind yourself of your pledge and commitment.*

forth time and energy) at overcoming your fear. This will include *actively learning* the techniques suggested in this handbook. However, you will not only passively read, but you will learn the techniques by pondering them, writing down your responses to the exercises, and then applying them to your life. Next, you will take time to diligently *practice* the techniques. You will even want to plan a practice schedule. Finally, you will need to *participate* in public communication (like classroom discussions) and deliver short speeches so you can put your knowledge and techniques to use, while developing public speaking skills.

If you are committed to overcoming your speechfright, if you get actively involved in reading, learning, and doing the exercises presented here, and if you diligently practice the anxiety-reduction techniques in preparation for giving speeches, you can become a calm and even confident speaker. Remember, athletes learn their skill not only by passively watching or reading about a sport, but also by practicing and participating in the game. You, too, must become an active participant in learning to overcome your speechfright and then in practicing public speaking skills.

CHAPTER SUMMARY

Deciding to take action to conquer your speechfright is the first step in overcoming it. This handbook will provide you with the tools you need to reach your goal. You are not alone in your fear of public speaking. Almost three out of every four people report an anxiety or nervousness about speaking in public. Learning to overcome speechfright is like learning a new sport or language. The important keys to your success include: commitment, active learning, practice, and participation. If you are committed to conquering speechfright, if you get actively involved in reading, learning and doing the exercises, if you practice the anxiety-reduction techniques, and then if you participate in public speaking opportunities, you will become a confident speaker.

REVIEW QUESTIONS

After reading this chapter, you should be able to answer the following questions:

1. When people are asked to rank their greatest fear, what do they often list?
2. How many years have communication scholars and educators spent researching how to help people overcome their fear of public speaking?
3. Learning to overcome speechfright can be compared to learning what other activities?
4. What are the four keys to conquering the fear of public speaking?
5. Who do you identify with most in this chapter—Christy or Trevor? Why?

CHAPTER TWO

DEFINITIONS AND ASSESSMENTS

"Speechfright" is one term, among many, that people use to describe their fear about public speaking. "Communication apprehension" (CA) is the academic term used by communication researchers to describe a fear or anxiety about communication. CA can be classified under four different types and self-assessed by level. The following chapter will help you understand the definitions and types of CA, as well as how to assess your CA levels and communication goals.

2.1 THE ACADEMIC DEFINITION: COMMUNICATION APPREHENSION (CA)

Communication apprehension (CA) is defined as "the fear or anxiety associated with real or anticipated communication with others" (McCroskey, 1977, p. 78). Although fear, anxiety, uneasiness, or nervousness about public speaking are words you may use interchangeably with the term speechfright, CA is the academic or scholarly term for speechfright. It is the term used most often in communication research and journal articles. CA is an emotional response that an individual can have toward communication.

If you can answer "yes" to either or both of these questions, you have experienced CA in a public speaking context:

1. Have you ever experienced fear and anxiety while simply *anticipating* you will be speaking in public? Yes __________ No__________
2. Have you ever experienced fear and anxiety while *delivering* a speech or *speaking* in public? Yes __________ No__________

❄ ❄ ❄

Sally, age 40, said: "I used to nervously anticipate giving a speech. The moment I heard about a speech assignment I could feel it in my body. My

Harcourt Brace & Company

stomach would start feeling sick about a week before the speech. I would not be able to sleep for at least two nights before the speech. On the day of my presentation, my entire body would start trembling and my stomach would be in knots. The moment I started to speak I could feel the intense fear, and my face would turn bright red. . . . I was so glad to hear that there's help for people like me. Communication apprehension can be conquered."

❄ ❄ ❄

2.2 FOUR TYPES OF COMMUNICATION APPREHENSION (CA)

Communication research identifies four types of CA:

1. traitlike,
2. context-based,
3. audience-based, and
4. situational (Richmond & McCroskey, 1995).

Public Speaking Context

Meeting Context

Context-based Communication Apprehension

Traitlike CA is a "relatively enduring personality-type orientation toward a given mode of communication across a wide variety of contexts" (McCroskey, 1984, p. 16). In other words, if you have traitlike CA, you experience anxiety in most situations where you might have to communicate with others—in one-on-one conversations, in interviews, in small groups, in public, and in almost every situation except with family members or a few close friends. About 20 percent of our population experience traitlike CA (Richmond & McCroskey, 1995).

Context-based CA is a consistently fearful response and orientation toward communication in a specific setting or context (McCroskey, 1984). There are four common contexts where CA can occur:

1. public speaking,
2. meetings,
3. group discussions, and
4. interpersonal conversations.

Group Discussion Context

Interpersonal Conversation Context

Context-based Communication Apprehension

The most prevalent form of context-based CA is a fear of public speaking (Richmond & McCroskey, 1995). People who experience context-based CA may feel it in some contexts but not in others. For example, you might experience anxiety about communicating in public, but not in interpersonal conversations or small group discussions.

Audience-based CA is "a relatively enduring orientation toward communication with a given person or group of people" (McCroskey, 1984, p.17). People who experience audience-based CA will feel anxiety when communicating with a specific person or group of people. For example, you might experience audience-based CA whenever you talk with a professor at college, a superior at work, or a particularly abrupt colleague. Most people feel apprehensive when communicating with at least some individual, so audience-based CA is quite common (Richmond & McCroskey, 1995).

Situational CA is an emotional response of an individual to communicating with another person or persons at a given time (McCroskey, 1984). It is usually short-lived or transitory; when the situation passes, the anxiety dissipates. Most people have experienced situational CA at least sometime in their lives. For example, you may have felt situational CA during an important job interview or while taking an oral exam.

Since speechfright is context-based CA, this handbook specifically addresses context-based CA in the public speaking context. The techniques presented here are designed to help you overcome public speaking apprehension. However, you may find that these techniques can also help you manage communication anxiety in meetings, group discussion, and interpersonal contexts.

2.3 ASSESSMENT OF COMMUNICATION APPREHENSION (CA)

So far you have learned that CA is based on an individual's emotions and feelings of anxiety or fear associated with communication. Most people have experienced at least situational-based CA or audience-based CA. However, some people also experience traitlike CA (across many situations, audiences, and times) or context-based CA (related to a particular setting or context). Although you could probably identify the contexts for your CA from the descriptions in the last section, it will be helpful for you to determine your level of CA by context, so you can monitor your progress over the next few weeks.

Professor James McCroskey has developed a survey to help people self-assess their CA levels. It is called the "Personal Report of Communication Apprehension" (PRCA-24), and it will produce five scores (Richmond & McCroskey, 1995). It will give you an *overall* or *traitlike* level of CA, as well as four context subscores—including *group discussions, meetings, interpersonal conversations, and public speaking.* Please complete the survey in Exercise 2.3 and then follow the directions for computing each of your five scores to assess your CA levels.

Exercise 2.3
Personal Report of Communication Apprehension (PRCA-24)*

Directions: This instrument is composed of twenty-four statements concerning feelings about communicating with other people. Please indicate in the space provided the degree to which each statement applies to you by marking whether you (1) strongly agree, (2) agree, (3) are undecided, (4) disagree, (5) strongly disagree. WORK QUICKLY; RECORD YOUR FIRST IMPRESSION.

___ 1. I dislike participating in group discussions.
(1) strongly agree (2) agree (3) are undecided (4) disagree (5) strongly disagree

___ 2. Generally, I am comfortable while participating in group discussions.
(1) strongly agree (2) agree (3) are undecided (4) disagree (5) strongly disagree

___ 3. I am tense and nervous while participating in group discussions.
(1) strongly agree (2) agree (3) are undecided (4) disagree (5) strongly disagree

___ 4. I like to get involved in group discussions.
(1) strongly agree (2) agree (3) are undecided (4) disagree (5) strongly disagree

___ 5. Engaging in a group discussion with new people makes me tense and nervous.
(1) strongly agree (2) agree (3) are undecided (4) disagree (5) strongly disagree

___ 6. I am calm and relaxed while participating in group discussions.
(1) strongly agree (2) agree (3) are undecided (4) disagree (5) strongly disagree

___ 7. Generally, I am nervous when I have to participate in a meeting.
(1) strongly agree (2) agree (3) are undecided (4) disagree (5) strongly disagree

___ 8. Usually, I am calm and relaxed while participating in a meeting.
(1) strongly agree (2) agree (3) are undecided (4) disagree (5) strongly disagree

___ 9. I am very calm and relaxed when I am called upon to express an opinion at a meeting.
(1) strongly agree (2) agree (3) are undecided (4) disagree (5) strongly disagree

___ 10. I am afraid to express myself at meetings.
(1) strongly agree (2) agree (3) are undecided (4) disagree (5) strongly disagree

___ 11. Communicating at meetings usually makes me uncomfortable.
(1) strongly agree (2) agree (3) are undecided (4) disagree (5) strongly disagree

___ 12. I am very relaxed when answering questions at a meeting.
(1) strongly agree (2) agree (3) are undecided (4) disagree (5) strongly disagree

___ 13. While participating in a conversation with a new acquaintance, I feel very nervous.
(1) strongly agree (2) agree (3) are undecided (4) disagree (5) strongly disagree

*Printed by permission from author, Dr. James C. McCroskey.

___ 14. I have no fear of speaking up in conversations.
(1) strongly agree (2) agree (3) are undecided (4) disagree (5) strongly disagree

___ 15. Ordinarily, I am very tense and nervous in conversations.
(1) strongly agree (2) agree (3) are undecided (4) disagree (5) strongly disagree

___ 16. Ordinarily, I am very calm and relaxed in conversations.
(1) strongly agree (2) agree (3) are undecided (4) disagree (5) strongly disagree

___ 17. While conversing with a new acquaintance, I feel very relaxed.
(1) strongly agree (2) agree (3) are undecided (4) disagree (5) strongly disagree

___ 18. I'm afraid to speak up in conversations.
(1) strongly agree (2) agree (3) are undecided (4) disagree (5) strongly disagree

___ 19. I have no fear of giving a speech.
(1) strongly agree (2) agree (3) are undecided (4) disagree (5) strongly disagree

___ 20. Certain parts of my body feel very tense and rigid while I am giving a speech.
(1) strongly agree (2) agree (3) are undecided (4) disagree (5) strongly disagree

___ 21. I feel relaxed while giving a speech.
(1) strongly agree (2) agree (3) are undecided (4) disagree (5) strongly disagree

___ 22. My thoughts become confused and jumbled when I am giving a speech.
(1) strongly agree (2) agree (3) are undecided (4) disagree (5) strongly disagree

___ 23. I face the prospect of giving a speech with confidence.
(1) strongly agree (2) agree (3) are undecided (4) disagree (5) strongly disagree

___ 24. While giving a speech, I get so nervous I forget facts I really know.
(1) strongly agree (2) agree (3) are undecided (4) disagree (5) strongly disagree

Scoring: To compute your scores merely add or subtract your scores for each item as indicated below. (Please note that "18" is a constant, so all your subscores will be computed by starting with a score of "18.")

Subscore (Context)	Scoring Formula
Group Discussions	**18 plus (+) scores for items 2, 4, & 6; minus (–) scores for items 1, 3, & 5.**
Meetings	**18 plus (+) scores for items 8, 9, & 12; minus (–) scores for items 7, 10, & 11.**
Interpersonal Conversations	**18 plus (+) scores for items 14, 16, 17; minus (–) scores for items 13, 15, & 18.**
Public Speaking	**18 plus (+) scores for items 19, 21, & 23; minus (–) scores for items 20, 22, & 24.**
Overall or Traitlike	**Add all four subscores together (Group Discussions + Meetings + Interpersonal Conversations + Public Speaking)**

Using the scoring formulas, please compute your five scores and write them in the following chart.

YOUR PRCA SCORES CHART

Overall & Context	Your Score	"x" Check Your Level		
		Low	Average	High
Group	______	______	______	______
Meetings	______	______	______	______
Interpersonal	______	______	______	______
Public Speaking	______	______	______	______
Overall	______	______	______	______

INTERPRETING: To interpret your scores, you can compare your scores with the thousands of people who have also completed the PRCA-24 (see Norms Chart).

NORMS CHART FOR THE PRCA-24

CONTEXT	AVERAGE SCORE	AVERAGE RANGE	HIGH CA SCORES
Group	15.4	11 to 20	21 & ABOVE
Meeting	16.4	12 to 21	22 & ABOVE
Interpersonal	14.5	10 to 18	19 & ABOVE
Public Speaking	19.3	14 to 24	25 & ABOVE
Overall	65.6	50 to 80	81 & ABOVE

The *overall score* can range from 24 to 120. The average overall score is 65.6, and the average range of scores is 50 to 80 (Richmond & McCroskey, 1995). If your overall score is near 65, then it is about normal. If it falls between 50 and 80, it may be a bit above average or below average but it is still within the normal range. If your overall score is above 80, you can conclude that you have a higher than average level of CA. If your overall score is below 50 than you can conclude that you have a lower than average level of CA.

Scores for each of the four contexts—group discussions, meetings, interpersonal conversations, and public speaking—can range from 6 to 30. Any subscore above 18 indicates you have some degree of communication apprehension in a specific context (Richmond & McCroskey, 1995). Notice that the average public speaking score is above 18, which indicates most people tend to be apprehensive about public speaking.

Now return to "Your PRCA Scores Chart" and check (x) the level for each of your scores in comparison to the norms. This chart will give you a good assessment of your overall CA level as well as your CA level in the four contexts.

Do your scores show that you need to use this handbook to learn the techniques to overcome CA? If so, keep reading. There is help for you in the following pages.

2.4 RESEARCH IN COMMUNICATION APPREHENSION

Did you know that some of the brightest and most talented people in the world—including Winston Churchill, John Fitzgerald Kennedy, Margaret Thatcher, Barbara Walters, Johnny Carson, and Barbra Streisand—once reported a fear of public communication (Ayers, 1994; Manchester, 1967; Seligmann & Peyser, 1994)? Students often say their fear of public speaking makes them feel stupid and less intelligent than others or even weak and cowardly. However, communication research shows that the fear of public speaking has nothing to do with a person's intelligence or talents. In fact, the fear of public speaking has nothing to do with your gender. Both men and women experience anxiety about public speaking.

❊ ❊ ❊

Kim, age 31, said: "I used to think that fearing to give a speech meant I was stupid or there was something wrong with me. . . . Both my husband and my sister like to speak in public so I thought I must not be smart enough to do that. . . . Now I know that even some of the brightest and most talented people in the world have feared giving a speech and have overcome their fear."

❊ ❊ ❊

Fearing to give a speech does not mean you are weak or cowardly or neurotic. Again, the communication research reveals that fear or anxiety about public speaking is not related to other kinds of nervous problems.

The communication research shows that the fear of public speaking *is* related to communication avoidance. Since we live in a society where communication is highly valued and a part of everything we do, it is very difficult to escape public communication. If you try to escape it, you could lose many opportunities to share your ideas with others. Often, many of these opportunities include important steps or hurdles that could help you reach your future goals. For example, a final grade could depend on an oral presentation of a project. A final job interview may include presenting your ideas before a panel of executives. Once on the job, a coveted promotion and salary increase could be tied to a position that includes speaking regularly to employees or on behalf of the company to community organizations. Avoiding public speaking in any of these situations can lead to losing the good grade you deserve, the job you really wanted, or the career promotion you were qualified to attain.

Public speaking opportunities also can present themselves in your social or community life. For example, as best man or maid of honor for a wedding, you could be asked to toast the bride or groom before a crowded room of people at the wedding reception. Avoiding that opportunity would leave a friend with a void that you could have filled with your love and respect. Speaking before a school board on behalf of a program needed by your child, speaking as a representative of a cause or organization you really believe in, speaking up for a political issue you espouse or a candidate you support are all worthy public speaking opportunities that you need to seize instead of avoid.

Now you know that fearing to give a speech is *not* abnormal. It is a problem that many have experienced and conquered. You, too, can conquer your fear and nervousness! Deciding to learn and practice the techniques to overcome your anxiety about public speaking is one of the best decisions you will ever make. It means that you are moving in a new and right direction to reach your professional, social, and academic goals.

Exercise 2.4 Evaluating Your Goals

Since we tend to avoid what we fear, your speechfright may have already caused you to avoid situations and opportunities that kept you from reaching important goals. Now is a good time to evaluate your future goals, as well as how a fear of public speaking has affected past goal attainment. Please <u>write out</u> answers to the following questions:

1. Have you ever avoided a course because it involved public speaking?

   Yes_________ No_________

2. Have you ever received a lower grade than you could have earned because you did not participate in class discussions or give an oral report?

   Yes_________ No_________

3. Have you ever avoided taking a job or leadership position because it involved public speaking?

   Yes_________ No_________

4. Has a fear of public speaking ever kept you from achieving your goals?

   Yes_________ No_________

5. List your academic, professional, and social goals that developing public speaking skills will help you attain.

   Academic Goals:

   Professional (Career) Goals:

   Social Goals:

Be encouraged; you no longer have to miss or redirect your goals because of a fear about public speaking. **Speechfright can be conquered.**

CHAPTER SUMMARY

In the academic research, speechfright is called communication apprehension (CA) in the public speaking context. There are four types of CA: traitlike; context-based; audience-based; and situational. The four most common contexts for CA include: public speaking, meetings, group discussions, and interpersonal conversations. The communication research shows that CA is not related to intelligence, gender, or neuroticism. However, research does indicate that people who experience CA do try to avoid public communication. Avoiding communication can impact your career, grades, and social life. Deciding to learn and practice the techniques to overcome your fear of public speaking means you are moving in the right direction to attain your academic, professional, and social goals.

REVIEW QUESTIONS

After reading this chapter, you should be able to answer the following questions:

1. What is the academic term and its definition for speechfright?
2. Define the four types of communication apprehension (CA).
3. Describe the four contexts where CA can occur.
4. Explain the difference between traitlike CA and public speaking CA.
5. What is the most prevalent form of context-based CA?
6. List three human characteristics that are NOT related to or associated with CA.
7. Explain why and how CA can impact a person's academic, professional, and social life.
8. What have you learned about yourself by completing the PRCA-24 and examining your experiences and goals?
9. What might you share with a person who told you they avoid public presentations either on the job or in a group discussion?
10. Who do you identify with most in this chapter—Sally or Kim?
    Why?

CHAPTER THREE

CAUSES OF SPEECHFRIGHT

Since you are reading this handbook because you want to overcome your fear of public speaking, you may be wondering what causes speechfright or why you experience it. Researchers have discovered a variety of causes for a person's fear of public speaking, and for some people, understanding what caused it is helpful. However, even if you never know what caused it, *communication research has shown that the major techniques for overcoming speechfright will work regardless of the cause.* For the purpose of understanding your speechfright, this chapter will explain six possible causes for a person's fear and anxiety about public speaking:

1. learned responses,
2. worrisome thoughts,
3. a performance orientation,
4. perceived lack of skills,
5. excessive activation or body chemistry, and
6. situational aspects of the circumstance or the audience.

3.1 LEARNED RESPONSES

Communication research points out two underlying causes for traitlike communication anxiety that can also apply to the public speaking context. These causes include **reinforcement** and **modeling,** which are learned responses (Ayres, 1988; Daly & Stafford, 1984; McCroskey, 1982, Van Kleeck & Daly, 1982).

Reinforcement theory points out that learned expectations cause behavior (Daly & Stafford, 1984; McCroskey, 1982). If children receive positive reinforcement for speaking (praise, pats on the head, smiles, or other rewards), they learn to associate positive consequences with communication. They learn to feel calm when speaking with others. On the other hand, if children are punished or given negative reinforcement when they speak at home or school, they quickly learn to associate communication with negative expectations. In order to avoid the aversive consequences, they avoid communication. Consequently, they develop a traitlike (overall) fear of communication. In addition, some children develop a learned helplessness from a random pattern of responses (some negative, some positive) to their communication (McCroskey, 1982). Eventually, they too learn to avoid speaking in many situations.

Reinforcement theory also applies to speechfright. If sometimes, even as a child, you received negative reinforcement in the form of laughter, negative evaluation, or punishment as a result of speaking in front of others, you could have learned a fear response to public speaking. You developed negative expectations in regard to speaking in public. Today, you may still be experiencing that same fear response. You may be reacting to those negative expectations for failure and embarrassment that you learned as a child or teenager.

❊ ❊ ❊

Jerry, age 26, wrote: "When I was in junior high, we had to give a five-minute speech for an English class. I was really scared because I had never given a speech. I spoke for only two minutes and left out half of what I planned to say. The teacher pointed out what a terrible job I did in front of everyone. The other students looked embarrassed for me. . . . Until now, I tried to avoid public speaking because it would only mean more criticism and failure for me. . . . I was glad to hear I could develop a new calming response to public speaking."

❊ ❊ ❊

Modeling or watching the reactions of others can also explain a learned fear response to communication (Bandura, 1973). Children learn behaviors by watching others as their models. If children see their parents constantly interacting and talking, they learn to interact and talk freely. However, the opposite also is true. If significant others in children's lives model cool, quiet, even fearful behaviors in regard to communication, children can learn to react in that way too.

In regard to public speaking fear, you may have learned to be afraid of public speaking by watching the reactions of others. If others whom you admired exhibited a fear of public speaking or if you perceived negative evaluation for those modeling public speaking, you may have learned to fear public speaking yourself.

THE GOOD NEWS is that even if your speechfright is a learned response to past situations, events, or environments, there are techniques you can learn to alleviate your speechfright. In other words, even *if you have learned a fearful response* to public speaking, *you will be able to learn a new calming response* to public speaking.

3.2 WORRISOME THOUGHTS

Worrisome thoughts (or cognitions) are another cause or driving force behind speechfright. According to Desberg and Marsh (1988), the number one cause of stage fright is fearful thoughts of negative evaluation and failure. Other researchers have shown that speechfright commonly arises when students think they cannot meet the expectations of their audience (Ayres, 1986). But when they learn that their audience is less difficult to please than first expected, their fears subside.

❊ ❊ ❊

Lyle, age 19, said: "In regard to public speaking, I always thought everyone was evaluating everything I did and every word I said. I thought no one would like what I have to say. At the very least, I would sound like an idiot or everyone would become bored. I saw the audience as a beast that I could not please. Since I knew I could never be a perfect speaker, I became even more terrified of public speaking. . . . I was glad to learn that most of those thoughts just were not true."

❊ ❊ ❊

Fear of negative evaluation and failure is rooted in your thought processes. If you think or mentally predict that you cannot live up to an audience's grand expectations, you will jump to all kinds of conclusions about the audience, the situation, and yourself. An irrational fear (not based on the possibility of physical harm) will grip your mind and nervous system. When you feel the nervous energy, you will use it to confirm your suspicions that the situation is fearful and to be avoided (Behnke & Beatty, 1981; Desberg and Marsh, 1988). Then your mind will continue to jump to all kinds of negative conclusions and distortions about how bad public speaking really is, how beastly the audience is, and what a fool you will be if you attempt a speech. The fear of becoming fearful will escalate and result in even more fear, nervousness, and avoidance of public speaking (Behnke & Beatty, 1981).

THE GOOD NEWS is that even if your speechfright is based in worrisome thoughts of negative evaluation and failure that escalate into even more fear (to the point of being fearful of the fear), there are techniques for alleviating speechfright that can help change your worrisome thoughts into positive coping statements. In other words, even if you have developed worrisome, fearful thinking patterns about public speaking, you will be able to learn new truthful, coping, calming, confidence-building thoughts.

3.3 PERFORMANCE ORIENTATION

Another explanation for the cause of speechfright is called a "performance orientation" (Motley, 1991, p.88). The performance orientation is related to worrisome thoughts of negative evaluation because it also involves thoughts and attitudes toward public speaking.

In the performance orientation, a speaker views public speaking as a situation demanding a perfect, aesthetic impression, elevated language, flawless oratorical skills or eloquence, and a formal, polished, brilliant delivery (Motley 1991). The performance orientation views the audience in a hypercritical evaluation mode that makes one small mistake unforgivable. These misconceptions about the formality and demands of public speaking increase worrisome and fearful thoughts, which, in turn, increase fear and nervousness.

❊ ❊ ❊

Michelle, age 18, wrote: "I used to think that public speaking meant I had to speak in a brilliant, flawless way. I knew everyone could give a better speech than me. I felt that if I said one wrong word or sounded boring, I would be an embarrassment. I was glad to learn that public speaking doesn't mean I have to perform eloquently or perfectly. I can be myself."

❊ ❊ ❊

Even if your speechfright is based on a performance orientation that demands formality and perfection to please a hypercritical audience, you can develop a **communication orientation** to public speaking. A communication orientation views public speaking as a communication encounter that relies on the ordinary communication skills that you use in everyday conversation (Motley, 1991). The focus is on helping the audience understand your message, not on audience scrutiny of every detail.

THE GOOD NEWS is that there are techniques for alleviating speechfright that will help you change a **performance orientation** into a **communication orientation**. A communication orientation will help you shift your thinking about public speaking from a formal speaker-centered performance to an audience-centered and message-focused communication encounter that in turn will help alleviate your fears and nervousness.

3.4 PERCEIVED LACK OF PUBLIC SPEAKING SKILLS

Another source of public speaking anxiety is **real or perceived lack of skills** (Richmond & McCroskey, 1995). Many people will tend to feel anxious when they do not know how to behave in a situation. Likewise, in a public speaking context, when speakers do not know what to do or say, fear and anxiety can increase.

❆ ❆ ❆

Chan, age 22, said: "I didn't know how to write a speech, let alone give one. Since English isn't my native language, not knowing what to say or do made my fear worse. . . . After I learned public speaking skills and what the speechmaking process was all about, I began to feel more confident."

❆ ❆ ❆

THE GOOD NEWS is that if a lack of public speaking skills causes your speechfright, you can learn and develop those skills. Effective public speaking skills are taught in all public speaking fundamentals courses, business and professional speaking workshops or classes, and in organizations devoted to presentational speaking. Since this handbook is designed as an auxiliary resource for a communication course, you are probably enrolled in a class or workshop where you can learn and develop your skills through practice. If you are not enrolled in a public speaking or communication course, then once you have practiced the techniques in this handbook, you should try to enroll in a class where you can learn and practice effective public speaking skills.

3.5 EXCESSIVE ACTIVATION OR BODY CHEMISTRY

Anxiety about communication has also been related to a person's excessive activation level or body chemistry. Research studies, especially involving children, have found that some children are more easily activated or stressed than others during daily routine activities (Kagan & Reznick, 1986; Kagan, Reznick, & Snidman, 1988). Consequently, children with a low activation level (and a low tolerance for uncertainty and stress) can become easily aroused in stressful circumstances and produce stress-related chemicals in their bodies.

Often they tend to avoid communication and socialization in order to stay calm and evade feelings of activation.

As an adult, you may experience excessive activation in your body when it comes to public communication. Excessive activation often makes a person feel out of control because it can bring on trembling hands and feet, dry mouth, nausea, blushing, tense muscles, pounding or rapid heartbeat, temporary memory loss, wavering voice, shortness of breath, nervous gesturing, or swallowing difficulty (Gilkerson, 1942; Pucel & Stocker, 1983; Richmond & McCroskey, 1995). Although physiological arousal is the source of the problem, it is exacerbated when you interpret or label this excessive activation as "bad" and thus try to avoid public speaking and the "bad" activation feelings whenever possible. Labeling public speaking and activation as "bad" actually increases public speaking anxiety.

THE GOOD NEWS is that even if your speechfright is related to excessive activation, body chemistry, and/or a desire to avoid those "bad" feelings, there are techniques you can learn to alleviate feelings of excessive activation. You can learn to reduce your physiological sensations so that giving a speech no longer arouses excessive nervousness or an overwhelmingly fearful response. **You can learn a new calming response to public speaking, and then you will be able to label a little activation as "normal" or "energizing."**

3.6 SITUATIONAL ASPECTS

Many aspects of a situation contribute to the amount of speech anxiety a person experiences. These situational causes of speech anxiety include **novelty, conspicuousness,** and **audience characteristics** (Daly & Buss, 1984).

Novelty. Novelty involves a situation that is unfamiliar, an audience that is unfamiliar, or a role that is unfamiliar. In regard to public speaking, if you are speaking in an unfamiliar environment, if you do not know the audience you will be addressing, or if you have seldom given a speech, you may experience a fear of the unknown and an anxiety about how to act. The reverse is also true. The more you participate as a public speaker, the more acclimated you will become to that role and the more you will feel at ease with any audience or situation. Your anxiety from novelty will wane.

Conspicuousness. Conspicuousness means attention is focused on something or someone. In the public speaking situation, it is the speaker who stands out from an audience. Although being at the center of attention at first might seem frightening, it also means that your ideas are being heard by others and not ignored. Since being conspicuous is part of public speaking, you can learn to enjoy being the center of attention and knowing that the audience is listening to your ideas. If you are experiencing increased speechfright because you are the center of attention, you can learn to see the situation as if you were speaking conversationally to a few friends who are attentively listening to your suggestions.

Audience characteristics such as size, status, similarity, and formality. Audience characteristics such as size, status, similarity, and formality can all contribute to a speaker's anxiety. The larger the number of people in an audience, the higher the status of the people in an audience, and the more dissimilar an audience is in age, gender, education, or culture, the more anxiety speakers feel. The more formal the situation seems, the more anxiety speakers report because formality often requires certain behaviors that allow for little deviation. As with novelty and conspicuousness, the more you participate in public

Exercise 3.6 Assessing the Causes of Your Speechfright

Since it is helpful to understand your speechfright before you learn to manage it, now is a good time to assess the sources of your speechfright. Sometimes speechfright develops at an age when you cannot recall what instigated it. On the other hand, often you can attribute your anxiety to specific instances. Please write out answers to the following questions in an effort to identify the sources of your fear about public speaking and to understand your speechfright:

1. *Learned Responses.* Can you think of a situation where you learned that speaking in public has negative consequences?

   Yes ____________ No ____________

   If yes, where and when?

   Can you think of people who may have modeled avoidance or a fear of public speaking that you learned to imitate?

   Yes ____________ No ____________

   If yes, what was each person's relationship to you and what did they model for you?

2. *Worrisome Thoughts.* Do you have worrisome thoughts about public speaking that include a fear of failure and negative evaluation by the audience?

   Yes ____________ No ____________

   If yes, describe them.

3. *Performance Orientation.* Do you view public speaking from a performance orientation perspective where you think you have to use flawless, elevated, and dignified language or a formal, polished, brilliant delivery to be an effective speaker?

   Yes ____________ No ____________

   Would you feel less anxious about public speaking if you viewed public speaking from a communication orientation that relies on your everyday conversational skills?

   Yes ____________ No ____________

4. *Perceived Lack of Skills.* Do you believe you lack the skills to be an effective public speaker?

   Yes ____________ No ____________

   Are you willing to enroll in a class, learn, and practice the skills needed to become an effective public speaker?

   Yes ____________ No ____________

5. *Excessive Activation.* Do you label public speaking as "bad" because you experience those "bad" feelings of excessive activation (nervousness)?

   Yes ____________ No ____________

   Are you willing to learn techniques to help you feel calm and energized when speaking in public?

   Yes ____________ No ____________

6. *Situational Aspects.* Have you ever experienced communication anxiety because of situational characteristics (novelty, conspicuousness, audience characteristics)?

   Yes ____________ No ____________

   Explain your answer.

speaking and learn public speaking skills, the more comfortable you will feel in front of any audience regardless of the formality, size, or audience constituents.

Again, there is **GOOD NEWS.** Even if your speechfright is increased with novelty, conspicuousness, or audience characteristics, applying the techniques in this handbook will help alleviate your speechfright in any situation. You will learn to manage your fear when speaking to a large number of people, a high-status audience, a dissimilar audience, or an audience in formal situations.

CHAPTER SUMMARY

Researchers have discovered a variety of causes for a person's fear of public speaking. These causes include 1) learned responses, 2) worrisome thoughts, 3) a performance orientation, 4) perceived lack of skills, 5) excessive activation, and 6) situational aspects of the circumstance or audience. However, THERE IS GOOD NEWS FOR EVERYONE. Although people often want to understand what caused their speechfright, it's NOT vital to discover the causes in order to find an effective treatment. The techniques presented in this handbook will help you overcome the fear of public speaking. They are supported by substantial communication research and have helped thousands of people reduce their fear and anxiety about public speaking regardless of the causes.

REVIEW QUESTIONS

After reading this chapter, you should be able to answer the following questions:

1. Why is it helpful but not essential to understand the causes of your fear and anxiety about public speaking?
2. What are six possible causes for speechfright?
3. Describe an example of a learned response cause of speechfright.
4. Explain the differences between reinforcement and modeling learned responses.
5. Identify the most common worrisome thoughts that increase speechfright.
6. If, as a speaker, you think you cannot meet your audience's expectations and then you feel nervous energy in your body, what is likely to happen next?
7. Compare and contrast the following views of public speaking: the performance orientation and the communication orientation.
8. How can someone alleviate speechfright caused from a perceived lack of public speaking skills?
9. What are some of the physiological symptoms of excessive activation?
10. Explain the three situational causes of speech anxiety.

CHAPTER FOUR

EXCESSIVE ACTIVATION AND THE FIGHT OR FLIGHT RESPONSE

Where does all your excessive activation (physical nervousness) come from, or how can your body chemistry be a source of speechfright? The "fight or flight response" is one explanation (Benson, 1975; Cannon, 1914). When you perceive that a situation is threatening, your brain will stimulate your nervous system to prepare your body for the impending danger. Your body will produce a series of biochemical reactions to energize you. This response is called the "fight or flight response" and was first described by Dr. Walter Cannon (1914) of Harvard Medical School.

4.1 RESPONDING TO A PERCEIVED THREAT

The fight or flight response is an innate involuntary response that was especially important for our primitive ancestors. It was an instinct that protected them from danger. When cave people perceived danger, their bodies produced large bursts of energy to fight off or flee from predators, invading enemies, or other environmental dangers. Today, thousands of years later, when we perceive a danger or frightening circumstance, our bodies still produce all the physical energy from the fight or flight response. If the energy is not expended, it results in excessive activation.

The "Fight or Flight Response" is defined as an innate biochemical response in our bodies. It is brought on when our minds perceive a real or imagined threat that triggers the brain to stimulate the sympathetic nervous system to prepare the body to fight or flee from the situation. The resulting physiological activation and sensations from the biochemical reactions in our bodies is often labeled "nervousness."

4.2 TRIGGERING NERVOUS SENSATIONS

The fight or flight response is elicited when we *perceive* a real or imagined threat. It doesn't matter whether the threat is a real beast or the imagined threat of a beastly audience listening to your speech. It is the *perception* of a problem, real or imagined, that

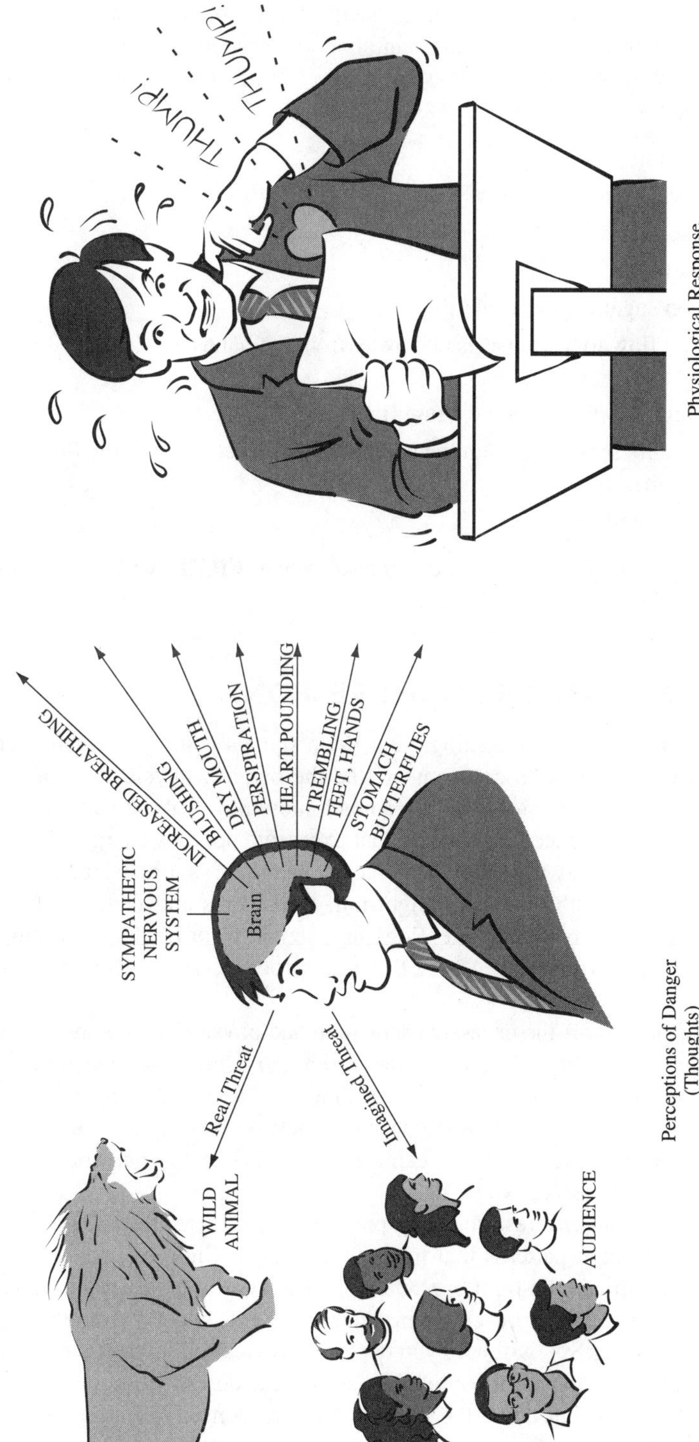

The Fight or Flight Response

triggers the hypothalamus (master stress-response switch in the brain) to stimulate the sympathetic nervous system (part of the autonomic nervous system) and the endocrine system to prepare the body to confront the physical danger. Some of the resulting physiological responses include:

1. increased heart rate;
2. increased blood pressure;
3. increased perspiration;
4. increased breathing;
5. increased blood sugar for more energy;
6. increased blood flow to the muscles and away from the hands and feet (causing them to feel cold);
7. locked diaphragm (indigestion and nausea);
8. increased adrenalin secretion (from the adrenal glands) that can stop the flow of saliva (dry mouth); and
9. trembling arms, hands, or feet.

All of these sensations are your body's response to prepare you to **FIGHT or FLEE** (Benson, 1975; Davis, Eshelman, & McKay, 1988).

4.3 HALTING THE FIGHT OR FLIGHT RESPONSE

If you perceive public speaking as threatening, your brain signals your sympathetic nervous system to prepare your body to confront or flee the danger. Physically, you are prepared to fight a wild beast or flee for your life—much more physical preparation than you need for giving a speech. Hence, you feel all that excessive nervous energy that can stymie your presentation, such as a pounding or racing heartbeat, shortness of breath, increased perspiration, dry mouth, nausea, indigestion, cold hands and feet, trembling hands and feet, wavering voice, blushing face, fidgeting, dizziness, or tingling sensations (Clevenger & King, 1961; Gilkerson, 1942; Pucel & Stocker, 1983; Richmond & McCroskey, 1995).

In order to counter or turn off the excessive activation and physical sensations of nervousness, you must stop the fight or flight response from activating. **You can halt the fight or flight response by** 1) stopping the worrisome thoughts that are alerting your brain to a threat or 2) calling forth relaxation to quiet the sympathetic nervous system and cause the parasympathetic nervous system to bring calm and equilibrium to your body again (Benson, 1975; Jacobson, 1938; Rice, 1987).

The technique called cognitive restructuring, presented in Chapter Seven, will help you stop the worrisome thought patterns that trigger the fight or flight response. When there is no perception of a threat, the fight or flight response will not be activated. In addition, systematic desensitization, presented in Chapter Eight, and deep abdominal breathing, presented in Chapter Six, will help you develop a relaxation response to public speaking. Since fear and relaxation are incompatible, systematic desensitization and deep abdominal breathing will help shut down the fight or flight response. When the fight or flight response is shut down, your excessive activation—including those aggravating

Exercise 4.3 Assessing Activation Sensations

1. Since the fight or flight response activates many of the following physiological sensations, please check (x) the ones that you experience before, during, or after you deliver a speech:

   __ Pounding or rapid heartbeat

   __ Blushing or red face

   __ Perspiring

   __ Shortness of breath

   __ Cold hands or feet

   __ Trembling hands or feet

   __ Nausea or indigestion

   __ Dizziness or tingling sensations

   __ Fidgeting or nervous gesturing

   __ Wavering voice

2. Please star (*) the nervous physiological sensations you experience when you *anticipate* the possibility of public speaking (refer to question #1 above).

3. Please mark (o) the nervous physiological sensations you experience when you *deliver* a speech (refer to question #1 above).

4. In summary, explain how the fight or flight response is causing your excessive activation, including all those nervous sensations.

nervous sensations (i.e., pounding heartbeat, nausea, trembling limbs, wavering voice, flushed face, dry mouth, increased perspiration)—will be minimized or eliminated.

CHAPTER SUMMARY

Excessive activation can be explained by the fight or flight response. The fight or flight response is an instinctive and involuntary response brought on by the perception of impending danger. When your brain perceives a threat, it triggers the body to stimulate the nervous system to release chemicals that prepare you to confront or flee the danger. These chemical reactions are responsible for many of your nervous sensations, such as increased heartbeat, increased perspiration, increased breathing, nausea, dry mouth, trembling limbs, cold hands and feet, and wavering voice. You can halt the fight or flight response by either stopping the worrisome thoughts that are alerting your brain to a threat or calling forth relaxation to quiet the nervous system. The techniques of cognitive restructuring, systematic desensitization, and deep breathing will inactivate or inhibit the fight or flight response. When the fight or flight response is inactivated, your nervous sensations will be minimized or eliminated.

REVIEW QUESTIONS

After reading this chapter, you should be able to answer the following questions:

1. How is excessive physical activation related to the fight or flight response?
2. Explain how the fight or flight response was an important and helpful response for primitive cave people.
3. Explain why the fight or flight response is *not* helpful for public speakers who perceive public speaking as a threatening situation?
4. List the nervous sensations triggered by the chemical reactions from the fight or flight response.
5. How can the fight or flight response be halted?
6. What techniques will help stop the fight or flight response?

Part 2

Treating Speechfright

CHAPTER FIVE

Overview of Approaches and Techniques

This book takes a combinational and multidimensional approach to treating speechfright (Dwyer 1995b). The combinational approach is based on recent communication research that shows the greatest reduction in public speaking anxiety is achieved when a combination of techniques are used rather than a single treatment (Allen, Hunter, & Donohue, 1989; Ayers & Hopf, 1993; Dwyer, 1995a; Rossi & Seiler, 1989; Whitworth & Cochran, 1996). The multidimensional approach is based on the multimodal counseling model (Lazarus, 1989) that emphasizes the importance of matching treatment techniques to each of seven human personality dimensions.

5.1 TECHNIQUES AND TREATMENTS IN THE COMBINATIONAL APPROACH

Seven treatment techniques, based on current communication research, as well as on stress management and counseling research, will be presented in this part of the text. These treatments include: deep breathing exercises, cognitive restructuring, systematic desensitization, mental rehearsal (visualization), physical exercises, interpersonal support, and skills training. The skills training technique will be explained only briefly because it is a major part of any public speaking course or business and professional speaking class. Anyone who desires to overcome speechfright eventually needs to enroll in a class where public speaking skills can be learned and practiced. A brief summary of the treatment techniques follows.

The **deep abdominal breathing** exercise is a "quick fix" to help reduce tension and bring on moderate relaxation within three to five minutes of any time you feel stressed. This exercise is also an initial part of two other important techniques, systematic desensitization and mental rehearsal. Deep abdominal breathing contributes to an oxygenated blood supply which is essential for good mental and physical health, whereas poorly oxygenated blood contributes to anxiety, depression, and fatigue (Davis, Eshelman, McKay, 1988).

Deep abdominal breathing exercises are based on the premise that it is difficult to be tense and to breathe deeply at the same time (Bourne, 1990). Since people who are fearful tend to breathe more shallowly from their chest, which only increases anxiety, deep breathing is an important activity to help decrease anxiety. When you have been trained to

Harcourt Brace & Company

breathe deeply from your abdomen, you will discover that your excessive activation symptoms from speechfright will start to subside. Since it is impossible to breathe deeply and be nervous at the same time, the fight or flight response of the sympathetic nervous system will be inhibited.

The **cognitive restructuring** (Meichenbaum, 1977) technique is based on the idea that people have worrisome, irrational, and nonproductive thoughts (cognitions) about themselves and their behavior. It is this illogical thinking that causes anxiety, fear, and nervousness. In order to reduce anxiety, fear, and nervousness, cognitions must be changed.

The cognitive restructuring technique when applied to speechfright trains individuals to recognize their worrisome cognitions and to replace them with more appropriate beliefs and positive coping statements. When your worrisome, irrational cognitions are displaced with calming, coping statements, your speechfright symptoms will diminish. The fight or flight response of the sympathetic nervous system will shut down.

The **systematic desensitization** (Wolpe, 1958) technique is based on learning theory. People learn to associate fearful responses with certain situations. In order to break the fearful response bond, people must learn a new relaxed response to the same situation.

The systematic desensitization technique trains individuals to achieve deep muscle relaxation and then to visually imagine the fear-producing situations. When you can visually imagine yourself in all the steps in the speechmaking process and maintain deep relaxation at the same time, you will have broken your fearful response to public speaking. You will have trained your body in a new relaxation response. You will notice that your excessive activation symptoms will diminish when you are in the public speaking situation. Since it is impossible to be relaxed and nervous at the same time, the fight or flight response of the sympathetic nervous system will shut down.

The **mental rehearsal** technique, also called visualization (Assagioli, 1973), is based on cognitive psychology. People have perceptions of an event that are connected to a mental image of the situation. If the mental image is negative, then anxiety or fear will be a natural response. On the other hand, if the image is positive, then positive feelings will occur. Athletes have long practiced this technique before a big event to improve their performance. Public speakers and writers have also found this procedure effective (Ayers & Hopf, 1985, 1991).

The mental rehearsal technique trains individuals to mentally rehearse a very positive speaking experience. You will begin picturing yourself on the day of your presentation arising from your bed, filled with confidence and energy, and then end by picturing yourself finishing a successful speech. When you have pictured yourself delivering a successful speech, you will have more positive feelings about that particular event. You will have less anxiety and will have prepared your mind for success.

Physical exercise is an effective way to reduce stress and anxiety. In fact, psychologists report that physical exercise is a good outlet for the body when it is aroused in the "fight or flight" state (Davis et al., 1988, p. 225). The United States Surgeon General and most medical and health organizations recommend a regular exercise program to maintain optimal health.

The brief physical exercise suggested in this text combines deep breathing with physical exertion, creating a "quick fix" prior to delivering a speech. When you exercise before giving a speech, you will feel less tension in your body. Medical experts unanimously suggest that you consider engaging in a regular exercise program as one way of reducing stress and tension in your life. This handbook does not recommend a particular exercise program because you should always consult your doctor before beginning any exercise program.

Interpersonal support involves having social relationships in our lives with people who can share our struggles and similar emotions or thoughts. Social support helps us manage stress in general, buffers its impact on our lives, and helps us stay committed to our goals as we feel a sense of commonality and encouragement. A public speaking class or special workshop on overcoming speech anxiety can provide a supportive environment where you can gain the confidence to learn and practice public speaking skills.

Skills Training (Fremouw & Zitter, 1978) is based on the idea that people fear public speaking because they lack delivery skills and do not know how to communicate in public. Obviously, everyone can become anxious or fearful about doing something new when they don't know how to do it or think they don't have the skills. The good news is that people can learn public speaking skills and reduce some of the fear of public speaking.

Skills training in public speaking teaches individuals how to research, outline, and deliver informative as well as persuasive speeches. One particular skills training program called "rhetoritherapy" emphasizes goal setting and analysis along with incremental skills training in several communication contexts (Kelly, 1989; Kelly, Duran, & Stewart, 1990; Phillips, 1977). Effective skills training in the public speaking context, based on the rhetoritherapy model, involves identifying a skill deficiency, setting an attainable goal, acquiring new skills, practicing the new skills in a nonthreatening environment, and then practicing the new skills in a natural environment. As you acquire public speaking skills in concert with applying the other techniques presented in this handbook, you will significantly reduce your anxiety, fear, and nervousness about public speaking.

5.2 THE SEVEN DIMENSIONS IN THE MULTIDIMENSIONAL APPROACH

The multidimensional approach emphasizes the importance of applying treatment techniques to each of the seven human personality dimensions (Dwyer, 1995b; Lazarus, 1989). The acronym BASIC ID (Lazarus, 1989) describes each dimension that can be involved in your speechfright:

1. **B**ehavior (inappropriate behaviors or lack of skills);
2. **A**ffect (fearful emotional feelings);
3. **S**ensation (excessive activation—nervous physiological feelings);
4. **I**magery (negative mental pictures or images);
5. **C**ognition (worrisome, irrational, or negative thoughts);
6. **I**nterpersonal Relationships (lack of interpersonal support systems); and
7. **D**rugs and Biological Functions (excessive stress on your physical well-being and/or use of harmful drugs) (Lazarus, 1989).

A more thorough description of each dimension will be presented in Chapter Eleven to help you learn how to pinpoint the source of your speechfright as a place to begin treatment. Keep in mind that it is important for you to carefully learn all of the techniques, because the combination of techniques will target all of your personality dimensions.

The **deep breathing exercises,** presented in Chapter Six, target the **affect** and **sensation** dimensions in order to induce relaxation and reduce stress in preparation for delivering a speech. **Cognitive restructuring,** presented in Chapter Seven, targets the **cognition** dimension, including the worrisome, irrational thoughts that produce a fear of public speaking. **Systematic desensitization,** presented in Chapter Eight, targets the **affect** (fearful emotional feelings), **sensation** (nervous physical feelings), and **imagery** (negative mental pictures) dimensions that are often at the heart of a heightened activation level and a learned fear response to public communication. **Mental rehearsal**, presented in Chapter Nine, targets the **imagery** and **cognition** dimensions in order to change your negative images as well as some of your uncertainty into positive perceptions and expectations for success. In addition, **physical exercise**, presented in Chapter Ten, targets the **drugs and biological functions** dimension in order to reduce stress in general, as well as prior to delivering a speech. **Interpersonal support,** also presented in Chapter Ten, targets the **interpersonal relationships** dimension and suggests building a support system of positive and confirming people that will help buffer stress, help you maintain commitment to your goals, and help you develop confidence and speaking skills in a supportive environment. Lastly, **skills training,** presented in Chapter Ten, targets the **behavior** dimension and suggests you enroll in a public speaking class or workshop where you can learn public speaking skills.

CHAPTER SUMMARY

This chapter presents an overview of the combinational and multidimensional approaches to treating speechfright. Communication research has shown that the combination of techniques (combinational approach) provides the greatest reduction of communication anxiety. The multimodal counseling model emphasizes the importance of matching treatments to personality dimensions (multidimensional approach). The seven treatments presented in this text include: deep abdominal breathing exercises, cognitive restructuring, systematic desensitization, mental rehearsal (visualization), physical exercises, interpersonal support, and skills training. Skills training will be only briefly explained because it is a major part of any public speaking course or workshop. The treatments presented target your seven personality dimensions involved in fear or anxiety: behavior, affect, sensation, imagery, cognition, interpersonal relationships, and drugs/biological functions.

REVIEW QUESTIONS

After reading this chapter, you should be able to answer the following questions:

1. What approaches does this text take to treating speechfright? Why?
2. List the techniques and exercises for treating speechfright that will be covered in this section of the text.
3. List the seven personality dimensions that require treatment in order to manage speechfright.
4. Explain the treatment or exercise that targets each dimension of your seven personality dimensions.
5. Based on what you read in this chapter, which technique(s) do you believe will be the most helpful to you? Why?

CHAPTER SIX

DEEP BREATHING EXERCISES

Breathing is so automatic that we take it for granted. We seldom think about it. However, breathing patterns can change and are directly related to the tensions carried in our bodies. For example, if you are anxious or fearful, your breathing will tend to be rapid and shallow, occurring high in your chest. If you are relaxed, your breathing will tend to be slow and deep, centering in your abdomen or midsection. A first step to quiet the fight or flight response of the sympathetic nervous system and reduce excessive activation from speechfright is to practice deep abdominal breathing. In addition, deep abdominal breathing is an important step in other speechfright-reduction techniques.

6.1 DEEP BREATHING INDUCES RELAXATION

Deep breathing targets the **affect** and **sensation** dimensions of your personality affected by speechfright. Deep breathing calms emotions and the bodily sensations from excessive activation. By stimulating your parasympathetic nervous system, the branch of your autonomic nervous system that promotes calm feelings and tranquility, deep breathing triggers relaxation. It helps shut off the fight or flight response.

Deep breathing uses your full lung capacity and is essential for good mental and physical health. It increases the oxygen supply to your brain and muscles. Thus, deep breathing can improve concentration and calm a racing mind. On the other hand, shallow breathing and poorly oxygenated blood actually contribute to anxiety, depression, and fatigue.

Deep breathing reduces the symptoms of hyperventilation, such as a rapid or pounding heartbeat, shortness of breath, dizziness, or tingly sensations. Hyperventilation involves extremely rapid breathing and exhaling too much carbon dioxide in relation to the amount of oxygen in your bloodstream (Bourne, 1990). It can occur when you are overly frightened and overbreathing through your mouth. Decreased carbon dioxide in your body can cause 1) your heart to pump harder and faster, 2) your brain to have increased constriction of blood vessels triggering feelings of dizziness or disorientation, and 3) your nerve cells to increase alkalinity eliciting jittery feelings (Bourne, 1990).

Fortunately, it is possible to change your breathing patterns. You can learn to control your breathing in order to prevent hyperventilation, to promote calmness, and to improve concentration. An initial step in controlling your breathing is to become aware of it.

Harcourt Brace & Company

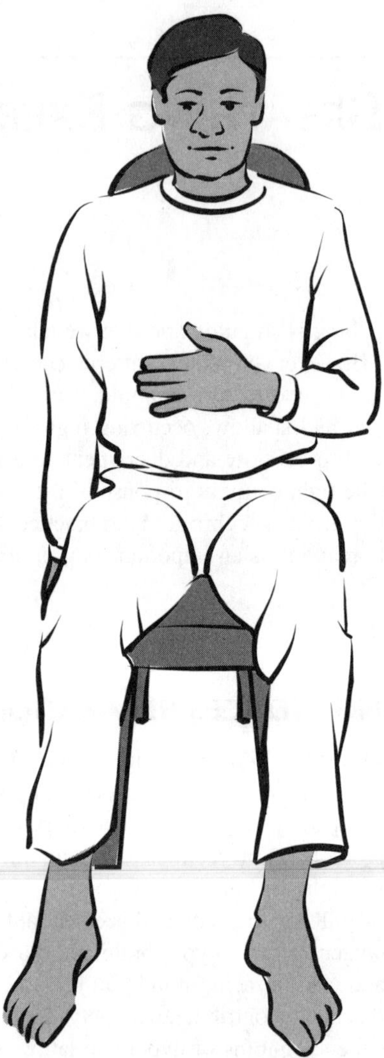

Place hand where breathing occurs

Breathing Evaluation

Exercise 6.1 Your Breathing Evaluation

Take a moment right now to evaluate your breathing. You will need to sit back in a chair or lie down on a flat surface with your legs straight out and your arms at your sides. Next, concentrate on your breathing for about a minute. Place one hand on the location that rises and falls as you breathe. Then, try to answer each of the following questions.

1. Does your breathing occur high in your chest (your chest rises when you breathe)?

   Yes______ No______

2. Does your breathing go deep down into your abdomen (your abdomen rises when you breathe)?

   Yes______ No______

3. Is you breathing rapid?

   Yes______ No______

4. Is you breathing slow and relaxed?

   Yes______ No______

5. Have you noticed any changes in your breathing patterns when you feel anxious, fearful, or stressed?

   Yes______ No______

6. Write a sentence to summarize your breathing.

NOTE: If you evaluated your breathing as rapid, shallow, or centered in your chest, you probably are not making good use of the lower part of your lungs. However, be encouraged because now you have identified a problem you can change. Your breathing can become relaxing, deep abdominal breathing that makes full use of your lung capacity. You can even learn to control it in stressful situations, such as right before delivering a speech.

6.2 DEEP ABDOMINAL BREATHING

Learning to breathe deeply from your abdomen is one of the first steps you can take to reduce your tenseness and physical symptoms of anxiety. As explained in Exercise 6.2, just three to five minutes of deep abdominal breathing can bring on moderate relaxation and shut off the fight or flight response (Bourne, 1990). Deep abdominal breathing is an important initial step in the Systematic Desensitization and Mental Rehearsal techniques, presented in Chapters Eight and Nine. In addition, it is a good "quick fix" to use in any tense situation. It can be easily practiced, unnoticed by anyone, while you are waiting your turn to give a speech. By learning and practicing deep breathing exercises you will be able to reduce tension in your body anytime because it is difficult to be tense and breathe deeply at the same time (Bourne, 1990). See Exercise 6.2.

❊ ❊ ❊

Jeff, age 26, said: "I could never calm myself before a speech until I discovered I was shallow breathing from my chest. Once I learned deep abdominal breathing, I started to relax before a presentation. It was a turning point in how I felt about public speaking."

❊ ❊ ❊

6.3 THE CALMING SIGH

Beyond the paramount deep abdominal breathing exercise, physicians and psychologists have suggested several breathing exercises to reduce stress. One quick exercise that public speaking students have reported helpful and tension-releasing while preparing for a speech is called the "Calming Sigh."

One of the signs that you are not getting enough oxygen or are experiencing some tension is your body's desire to sigh or yawn (Davis et al., 1988). A sigh is your body's way to relax and release tension. The calming sigh exercise can help trigger relaxation and relieve feelings of tension or nervousness. See Exercise 6.3.

CHAPTER SUMMARY

Deep breathing targets the affect and sensation dimensions of your personality. It can calm your emotions and physiological sensations of excessive activation, improve your concentration, and reduce the symptoms of hyperventilation. The deep abdominal breathing exercise is a quick fix you can use anytime you feel tense. Also, it is the initial step in both the systematic desensitization and the mental rehearsal techniques presented in later chapters. You can train yourself to use deep abdominal breathing by practicing the exercise for three to five minutes per day for about two weeks. The calming sigh is a breathing exercise that releases tension and is especially helpful in preparation for delivering a speech.

REVIEW QUESTIONS

After reading this chapter, you should be able to answer the following questions:

1. Which personality dimensions does the deep abdominal breathing exercise target?
2. Explain hyperventilation and how to stop its symptoms.
3. List the benefits of practicing the deep abdominal breathing exercise.
4. What innate response do the deep breathing exercises shut off?
5. How can you train yourself in deep abdominal breathing?
6. Explain how to practice the calming sigh.
7. Now that you have repeatedly tried deep abdominal breathing and the calming sigh, explain how these experiences have helped you relax.

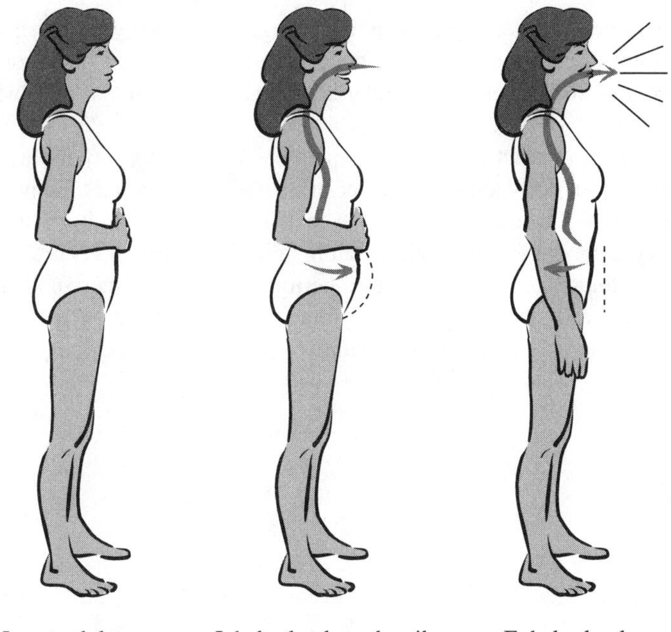

Locate abdomen	Inhale slowly and smile	Exhale slowly

Deep Abdominal Breathing Exercise

Exercise 6.2 Deep Abdominal Breathing Exercise

You can train yourself to use deep abdominal breathing by practicing this exercise daily for three to five minutes at a time. You can choose to stand or sit during the exercise. It is more relaxing if you practice it while sitting. (Actually, you can practice this exercise lying down with knees bent and your feet spread comfortably. But if you are tired and fall asleep, you will miss the practice session!) Follow these steps:

1. **First, scan your body and note if you are feeling any tension or anxiety.**
2. **Next, find your rib cage and place one hand directly below your rib cage—that is, your abdomen.**
3. **Now, concentrate on your breathing. Inhale *slowly and deeply* through your nose, feeling your abdomen expand and your hand rise for a count of four (1—2—3—4—). Your chest should barely move.**
4. **Pause slightly and smile for a count of four (1—2—3—4—). Smiling releases endorphins (natural mood elevators) into your blood.**
5. **Then, exhale slowly and fully through your mouth, making a "whoooo" sound like the blowing wind, for a count of four (1—2—3—4—).**
6. **Relax and take a few normal breaths. Tell your muscles to go loose and limp. Make an effort to let all the tension drain away from every part of your body.**
7. **Continue taking at least fifteen to twenty deep breaths with slow, full exhales for about three to five minutes.**

When you practice deep abdominal breathing, try to keep your breathing smooth and regular. Try not to gulp the air. If you get a little lightheaded at first, from the increased supply of oxygen, simply return to regular breathing for a minute or two and the lightheadness will subside.

You will want to practice deep abdominal breathing every day for at least two weeks in order to train your body to master the technique. After the initial training, you will find it an indispensable tool to use whenever you feel anxious or tense. It will trigger relaxation and especially help you feel calm right before you give a speech. You can adjust the deep abdominal breathing exercise so it can be performed without others noticing. Simply follow the same procedures, except exhale slowly and fully through your nose, instead of making the wind sound through your mouth.

Exercise 6.3 The Calming Sigh Exercise*

The calming sigh is an easy breathing exercise that helps trigger relaxation and relieve feelings of tension or nervousness. It is like a quiet yawn that gently opens the air passages. Follow these steps:

1. **Sitting or standing, simply sigh ("ahhhhh") gently but deeply and let the air flow naturally out of your lungs. (Just breathe in naturally and then exhale slowly and completely while sighing.)**

2. **Then, tell your body to go limp and to RELAX.**

The Calming Sigh can be used anytime you feel tense. You might find it helpful to practice the calming sigh a few times before starting the deep abdominal breathing exercise. Students have reported that practicing the calming sigh first and then following it with the deep abdominal breathing exercise is an especially good tension-reduction routine to use immediately before delivering a speech.

*The calming sigh exercise is an adaptation of the "Relaxing Sigh" suggested by Davis, Eshelman, & McKay, 1988.

CHAPTER SEVEN

COGNITIVE RESTRUCTURING

The cognitive restructuring technique is based on the premise that anxiety and fear are generated when people think fearful and negative thoughts about themselves and their behaviors (Meichenbaum, 1977). The goal of this technique is to help you change your thinking in order to change your anxious, fearful feelings. Cognitive restructuring targets the cognitive dimension of your personality.

The term "cognitive restructuring" (CR) is used to describe this technique because cognitive refers to cognitions (your thoughts), and restructuring means to systematically rebuild or remake. Thus, cognitive restructuring means you will learn to rebuild your thoughts about public speaking. The technique involves four steps and can result in a significant reduction in your fear and anxiety about speaking in public.

Cognitive restructuring (CR) involves these steps:

1. Discovering and creating a list of your worrisome thoughts, negative self-talk, and fearful beliefs about speaking in public
2. Identifying those worrisome, fearful thoughts and negative self-statements as irrational beliefs
3. Developing a list of positive coping statements to replace those irrational beliefs
4. Practicing the new coping statements until they almost automatically replace your old irrational beliefs

7.1 THE FIRST STEP: CREATING YOUR ULTIMATE FEARS LIST

The first important step in the cognitive restructuring technique is to discover your fearful thoughts about public speaking so you can change them. In order to accomplish this step, you need to develop your own ***"Ultimate Fears List"*** about public speaking. Please follow the directions for Exercise 7.1 before you read any further. **DO NOT SKIP THIS EXERCISE.** It is an essential part of learning the cognitive restructuring technique.

Example: Kim's Ultimate Fears List

Fear #1: I am afraid I will make a mistake. My speech will be ruined. I will be embarrassed and look stupid.

Fear #2: I can't stand public speaking because everyone is watching me. I am afraid that people will be judging everything I do and say.

Fear #3: Public speaking is terrible because I will look like a fool when I try to perform in a formal way.

Fear #4: I am afraid everyone will see how nervous I am. When I blush or shake or my voice cracks, the audience will laugh at me and think poorly of me.

Fear #5: Once I forgot important points. Now I worry I will get so nervous that I will go blank and forget everything.

Fear #6: Nervous feelings are awful, therefore public speaking is awful. I should feel calm in order to be a good speaker. I should never feel nervous.

Fear #7: The audience will think my speech is boring and will not be interested in what I have to say.

Fear #8: I am afraid I will speak so fast that the audience won't be able to understand me.

Fear #9: I am afraid I will lose control, hyperventilate, or faint.

Fear #10: I am afraid someone will ask a question I can't answer.

Others: I don't have any skills when it comes to public speaking. I don't know what to do or say.

7.2 STEP TWO: IDENTIFYING IRRATIONAL BELIEFS AND DISTORTIONS ON YOUR LIST

The second step in cognitive restructuring is to identify those worrisome thoughts on your list that are irrational, illogical, and unproductive. It is your irrational beliefs that are the core of your fear.

Irrational Beliefs vs. Rational Beliefs. Cognitive psychologists tell us that the cause of all anxiety and irrational fear is our irrational beliefs (Ellis & Harper, 1975; Ellis & Dryden, 1987). *Irrational beliefs* are evaluative thoughts that are rigid and stymieing and keep you from reaching your goals. They are *illogical* and *unrealistic* because they are not related to a perilous event or personal harm (Ellis & Dryden, 1987). They are *unproductive* because they keep you from achieving your goals and purposes.

On the other hand, *rational beliefs are logical and realistic beliefs that help you achieve your goals.* Rational beliefs involve concern for the well-being of yourself and others, but they are not inhibiting or immobilizing (Dryden & DiGiuseppe, 1990). Actually, they motivate you to engage in self-enhancing behaviors. For example, rational concern (or

Exercise 7.1 Your Ultimate Fears List

Imagine that you have just been assigned to give a speech to your class or another large group of people, and then answer these questions:

1. What fearful, worrisome, and nervous thoughts do you have? (I.e., what makes you nervous about public speaking?)

2. What negative self-statements come to mind? (I.e., what negatives do you say to yourself about yourself?)

Using the space below, list your biggest fears, worries, and negative thoughts about delivering a speech. List as many as you can. Later in this chapter you will be using "Your Ultimate Fears List" to create truthful coping statements. **So please, before going further, carefully complete this list.** (For an example, see Kim's Ultimate Fears List on the following page.)

Fear #1:

Fear #2:

Fear #3:

Fear #4:

Fear #5:

Fear #6:

Fear #7:

Fear #8:

Fear #9:

Fear #10:

Other fears or worries:

rational non-stymieing fear) causes you to take shelter when you hear a tornado warning or to protect your car when you hear a hailstorm is approaching. Rational concern leads you to discourage a friend from driving when he or she has been drinking. Rational concern about failing an important exam causes you to set aside enough time to study so you can earn a good grade. It just makes sense to be concerned about potential danger or injury. The human emotion of concern is crucial to your survival and part of your basic nature.

Rational concern becomes a problem when it becomes irrational, immobilizing fear and anxiety (Ellis & Dryden, 1987). It is irrational fear and negative thoughts that are often at the core of public speaking anxiety. Irrational fear about public speaking is a result of projecting harm and danger into a situation that is neither harmful nor dangerous. Although you may feel fearful about public speaking, logically, there is no potential danger in the event. If you think about it, have you ever heard of anyone getting killed or dropping dead from giving a speech? Public speaking is not a perilous or life threatening event! *It is your irrational beliefs about public speaking that are causing your fear, anxiety, and nervousness.*

The ABCDs of Irrational Fear and Anxiety. The ABCDs of irrational fear and anxiety further teach us that at the heart of speechfright is irrational beliefs (Ellis & Dryden, 1987).

The ABCDs of Irrational Fears*

"A" stands for the Activating Event, like public speaking, that arouses or activates your fear and anxiety.

"B" stands for your Beliefs (irrational fearful beliefs) about the activating event.

"C" stands for the Consequences (emotional consequences like anxiety, fear, or nervousness that are unproductive and inhibiting) you feel about the Activating Event.

"D" stands for Disconnecting your irrational fearful Beliefs about the Activating Event (public speaking) in order to eliminate your Consequences of anxiety, fear, and resulting nervousness.

*The ABCDs of Irrational Fears are based on the ABCs of Ellis and Dryden's (1987) rational emotive therapy .

It is not the **A=activating event** that causes the **C=consequences of fear and anxiety**. Otherwise, everyone would feel the same about the same event. But they don't! For example, why is it that one student feels that giving a speech is a fun, enjoyable, and invigorating experience while another feels it is a dreadful nerve-wracking occasion to be avoided? It is not the event of public speaking that causes nervousness and anxiety, or both students would feel the same. It is the **B=beliefs** about the event that cause one student to feel fearful or anxious while another student feels enthused and happy. If you want to get rid of your anxiety, nervousness and fear about the **A=activating event (i.e., public speaking)**, you need to **D=disconnect** (change) your irrational beliefs. So the ABCDs are an acronym to remind us to disconnect the irrational beliefs in order to eliminate irrational fear.

Irrational Beliefs Are Based on Must Thoughts. Research in the communication field shows that the fear of public speaking often includes irrational beliefs such as the following.

> **"My audience will be evaluating every little detail about me and every word I say. Therefore, I must give a perfect performance. I must not make any mistakes."**

These irrational beliefs are called "**MUST THOUGHTS" or "MUSTURBATORY THOUGHTS**" (Ellis & Dryden, 1987). Must thoughts are all the unrealistic things you tell yourself you ***MUST*** do. They are also called musturbatory thoughts because they are all the "musts" that you let disturb you. All the perfectionist demands you tell yourself fit into this category. They include all the "shoulds," "ought tos," "have tos" and "musts" you demand of yourself, others, and your situations. They result in negative self-statements and distorted thinking. They are responsible for your fear, anxiety and nervousness about public speaking. **Now complete Exercise 7.2a to determine which "must thoughts" apply to you.**

Exercise 7.2a Must Thoughts (Unrealistic Demands) List

Please place an "x" by the must thoughts that apply to you.

___ 1. **Do you think MUST THOUGHTS ABOUT YOURSELF?** Must thoughts about yourself, as a public speaker, can include:

If I speak in public, I must say just the right thing. I must never make a mistake. I must make a good impression. I must be perfect. I must always appear completely in control and sound intelligent. If I ever say the wrong thing, make a mistake, or look nervous, it will be awful, and I won't be able to bear it. People will think I am a fool. I will look incompetent and incapable.

___ 2. **Do you think MUST THOUGHTS ABOUT OTHERS?** Must thoughts about others in a public speaking situation can include:

Everyone in my audience must be judging every detail about my speech and my life. Everyone must like me. Everyone must like what I have to say and think my speech is really good. No one should ever become bored from my speech. If everyone doesn't like me and what I have to say or if anyone looks bored or disinterested, I will be a despicable person and a failure.

___ 3. **Do you think MUST THOUGHTS ABOUT SITUATIONS?** Must thoughts about public speaking situations include:

I must never give a speech unless the situation is perfect and I feel completely calm. If the situation is not perfect or if I don't know absolutely everything about a topic or if I feel nervous, I must NOT give a speech. Public speaking is an awful situation, and I must avoid it. I could be a failure and look like an idiot.

Did you find your thoughts in the exercise? The problem with must thoughts is they are rigid, dogmatic, perfectionistic, and unrealistic demands you make on yourself. They are irrational because they give you anxiety, immobilize you, and prevent you from achieving your goals. When you can not meet your "must" demands, you give yourself and others a negative evaluation and soon generate more self-defeating thoughts.

Rational Beliefs Include a Communication Perspective. Rational beliefs are the opposite of must thoughts. They include desires, preferences, or wishes (Ellis & Dryden, 1987). Rational beliefs are not dogmatic, like irrational beliefs. These thoughts do not demand perfection. For example, a rational belief says:

> **I want to give a good speech, but if I make a mistake or everyone doesn't appreciate what I have to say, or if I don't get a perfect grade, I will still like myself. I will have helped some people. I will offer what I can. I will be satisfied with a respectable job.**

Rational beliefs view public speaking from a communication perspective, not a performance perspective. A ***communication perspective*** (or orientation) sees public speaking as a communication encounter in which you have an opportunity to share your ideas with others (Motley, 1991, 1995; Motley & Molloy, 1994). *It relies on the same basic communication skills you use daily with family and friends.* On the other hand, a ***performance perspective*** (or orientation) sees public speaking as a performance that requires flawless oratorical skills, eloquence, and perfection in order to be effective and please a hypercritical audience. In the communication perspective your goal is to help your audience understand your message (Motley, 1991). Like everyday conversation, you can use the same natural delivery that you use when talking to a respected friend. *You can be yourself; you do NOT have to be perfect.*

A communication perspective sees an audience as fellow classmates or fellow members of the human race. They are not hypercritical or one gigantic ear waiting to criticize you for the least mistake. Members of your audience are like you when you listen to a speaker. They want to hear your message. They are not judging every word you speak. They are simply looking for ideas to help them in some way or to enrich their lives.

A rational belief about public speaking includes a communication perspective, not a performance perspective. A rational belief is *NOT dogmatic or perfectionistic* about yourself, your delivery, or your audience.

Must Thoughts Lead to Irrational Conclusions. Rational beliefs and irrational beliefs lead to different conclusions. *Rational beliefs are flexible* and do not escalate into dogmatic musts; they help you reach your goals (Dryden & DiGiuseppe, 1990). On the other hand, *irrational beliefs involve must thoughts that demand perfection, which is impossible for any human being* to achieve. The problem with must thoughts is that they lead to irrational conclusions that heighten fear, anxiety, and nervousness.

Irrational conclusions are stymieing and keep you from reaching your goals or from devising new ones. Irrational conclusions include **awfulizing, I-can't-stand-it-itus, damnation thinking, and always-and-never-thinking** (Ellis & Dryden, 1987; Dryden & DiGiuseppe, 1990). **Awfulizing** means that you conclude some event is 100 percent awful and worse that it should be. **I can't-stand-it-itus** means you conclude a particular event is so horrible that it cannot be endured. **Damnation thinking** means you are excessively critical and conclude you are a "damnable person" because you cannot live up to the perfection you and others expect or the audience is damnable because they expect perfection from you. **Always-and-never thinking** insists on absolutes and concludes situations will always be the same; they can never change and past experiences will always predict the future. In Exercise 7.2b, you will check the list of irrational conclusions about public speaking to see which ones apply to you.

Exercise 7.2b Irrational Conclusions about Public Speaking

As you read through the following questions and descriptions, *please place an "x"* by the irrational conclusions that you have about public speaking.

____ 1. Do you practice ***awfulizing?*** Do you believe that public speaking is 100 percent awful, bad, and worse than it ever should be? If you do, that's awfulizing from the must thoughts you demand of situations and yourself.

____ 2. Do you have ***I-can't-stand-it-itus?*** Do you believe public speaking is so horrible that you can NOT endure it; you can find NO happiness whatsoever if you hear you have to give a speech? If you do, that's an I-can't-stand-it-itus conclusion.

____ 3. Do you engage in ***damnation thinking?*** Do you excessively criticize yourself or others? Instead of admitting that you are a fallible human who can make a mistake, do you label yourself as stupid or worthless because you can't give a flawless speech? Instead of acknowledging that not everyone will like you, are you damning yourself or your audience because some might not appreciate your speech, interests or ideas? If you do, that's damnation thinking about yourself and others.

____ 4. Do you employ ***always-and-never thinking?*** Do you rigidly believe or predict that you will always forget some part of your speech because you did in the past? Do you believe you will never become a good public speaker? Do you tell yourself you will always be a shy person or an incompetent speaker? If you do, that's always-and-never-thinking about yourself and your future.

Must Thoughts Lead to Cognitive Distortions. These four irrational conclusions—awfulizing, I-can't-stand-it-itus, damnation thinking, and always-and-never-thinking—are linked to fear, anxiety, and goal defeat. They will not enhance your behavior or help you meet challenges, but instead, will lead to more negative self-talk and cognitive distortions.

Must thoughts not only lead to irrational conclusions, but also lead to cognitive distortions. Cognitive distortions are the unrealistic and negative thoughts that are not true but can sway your thoughts about positive experiences (Burns, 1980; Ellis & Dryden, 1987). They include negative self-statements or self put-downs. Cognitive distortions about public speaking include peephole thinking, ignoring the positive, psychic reading, microscopic viewing, emotional reasoning, all-or-nothing categorizing, labeling, personalizing, phonyizing, and perfectionizing. In Exercise 7.2c, you will check the list of cognitive distortions about public speaking to see which ones apply to you.

Exercise 7.2c Cognitive Distortions List

As you read through the following definitions, please place checks by the distortions that you have about public speaking.

___ 1. *Peephole Thinking* looks through a little hole in the door and focuses on one negative detail, to the exclusion of all other information. Your entire vision of the situation becomes clouded with the one negative. In public speaking, for example, you may receive many positive comments about a speech or topic, but you focus on the one small criticism or mistake. **The Truth: You can direct your attention to positive messages and to presenting your message. Although you can learn from constructive suggestions, you need not focus on past mistakes, criticisms, or fears.**

___ 2. *Ignoring the Positive* ignores all positive experiences, accomplishments, or compliments from others. In public speaking, for example, you may reject praises from others about your ideas. Instead, you choose to feel unworthy and inadequate as a public speaker because you forgot some detail. **The Truth: You have had successful experiences in life. Successes and compliments are encouraging and worth relishing. Focusing on past shortcomings or failures will not foster goal attainment.**

___ 3. *Psychic Reading* presumes to predict the future and read others' minds. You presume everyone will be negative or that you will make a mistake and do poorly. In public speaking, for example, you might notice an audience member yawning. He has worked all night or crammed for an exam, but as a psychic reader, you falsely presume, "My audience is bored and disinterested." **The Truth: You cannot predict the future or read another's mind. If you prepare your speech and outline, you will have notes to guide you. If you make a mistake or forget a part, you can refer to your notes and keep going. You will contribute something by sharing your ideas. (Psychic Reading might be profitable if you buy a crystal ball and a 900 number, but it will not help you conquer your fear of public speaking. It is merely a false presumption.)**

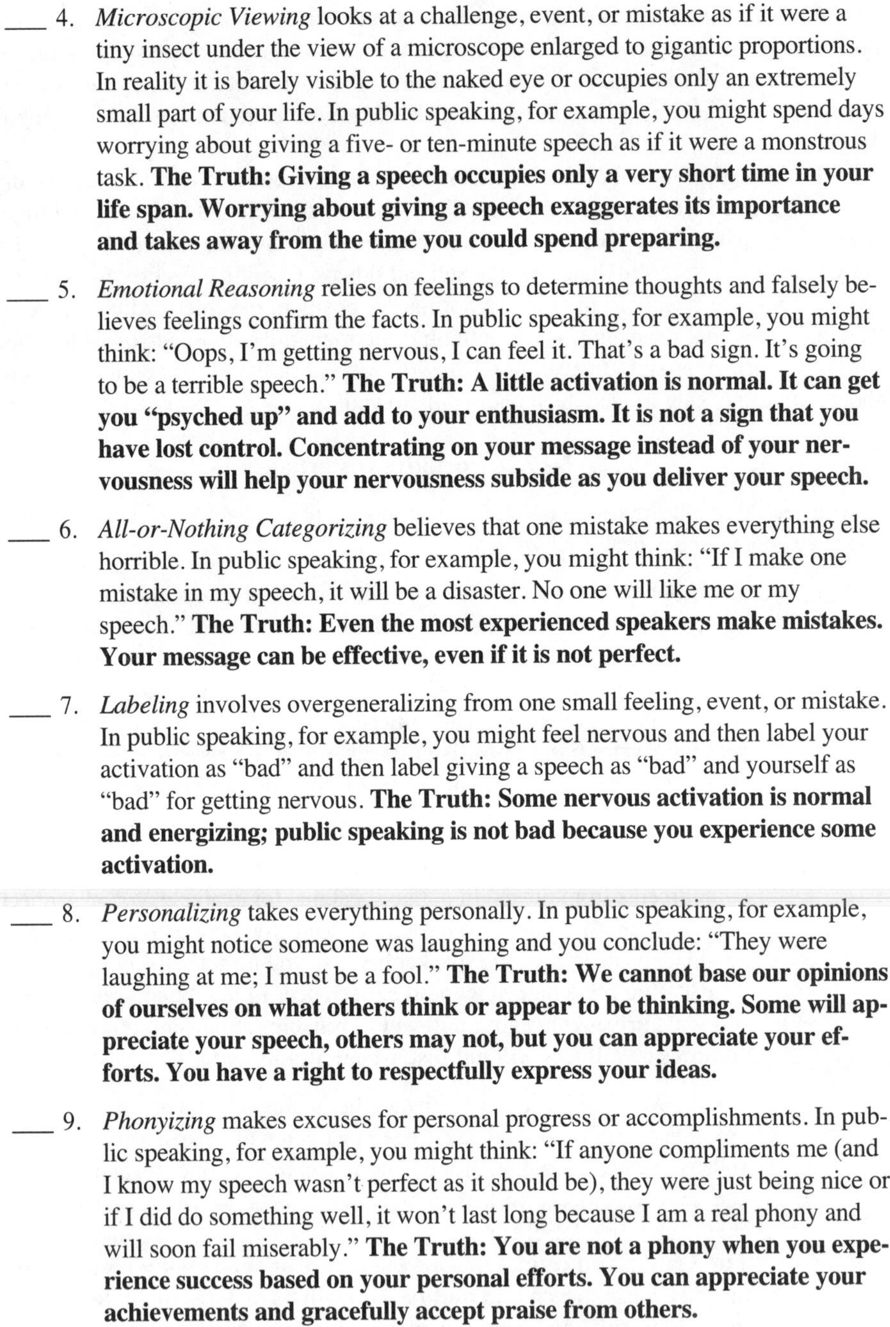

___ 4. *Microscopic Viewing* looks at a challenge, event, or mistake as if it were a tiny insect under the view of a microscope enlarged to gigantic proportions. In reality it is barely visible to the naked eye or occupies only an extremely small part of your life. In public speaking, for example, you might spend days worrying about giving a five- or ten-minute speech as if it were a monstrous task. **The Truth: Giving a speech occupies only a very short time in your life span. Worrying about giving a speech exaggerates its importance and takes away from the time you could spend preparing.**

___ 5. *Emotional Reasoning* relies on feelings to determine thoughts and falsely believes feelings confirm the facts. In public speaking, for example, you might think: "Oops, I'm getting nervous, I can feel it. That's a bad sign. It's going to be a terrible speech." **The Truth: A little activation is normal. It can get you "psyched up" and add to your enthusiasm. It is not a sign that you have lost control. Concentrating on your message instead of your nervousness will help your nervousness subside as you deliver your speech.**

___ 6. *All-or-Nothing Categorizing* believes that one mistake makes everything else horrible. In public speaking, for example, you might think: "If I make one mistake in my speech, it will be a disaster. No one will like me or my speech." **The Truth: Even the most experienced speakers make mistakes. Your message can be effective, even if it is not perfect.**

___ 7. *Labeling* involves overgeneralizing from one small feeling, event, or mistake. In public speaking, for example, you might feel nervous and then label your activation as "bad" and then label giving a speech as "bad" and yourself as "bad" for getting nervous. **The Truth: Some nervous activation is normal and energizing; public speaking is not bad because you experience some activation.**

___ 8. *Personalizing* takes everything personally. In public speaking, for example, you might notice someone was laughing and you conclude: "They were laughing at me; I must be a fool." **The Truth: We cannot base our opinions of ourselves on what others think or appear to be thinking. Some will appreciate your speech, others may not, but you can appreciate your efforts. You have a right to respectfully express your ideas.**

___ 9. *Phonyizing* makes excuses for personal progress or accomplishments. In public speaking, for example, you might think: "If anyone compliments me (and I know my speech wasn't perfect as it should be), they were just being nice or if I did do something well, it won't last long because I am a real phony and will soon fail miserably." **The Truth: You are not a phony when you experience success based on your personal efforts. You can appreciate your achievements and gracefully accept praise from others.**

____10. *Perfectionizing* believes a speaker must be perfect, look perfect, and never make a mistake in order to be acceptable. In public speaking, for example, you think: "No one should ever see me sweat, stumble, shake, or blush. If I cannot look really good or give a perfect speech, I will be a complete failure." **The Truth: No one will ever be perfect in this life. We are all fallible humans who make mistakes. You can accept yourself and be satisfied with giving your best effort.**

(These distortions are based on general classifications of cognitive distortions and illogicalities suggested by Beck, Rush, Shaw, & Emery [1979], Burns [1980], and Ellis & Dryden [1987].)

How many of the distortions apply to you? Three? Four? Five? All of them? When you think must thoughts that demand perfection of yourself, you will irrationally believe that your audience requires perfection in order to get anything out of your speech. Your thoughts will continue to be flooded with distortions and more negative self-statements.

7.3 STEP THREE: DEVELOPING A LIST OF POSITIVE COPING STATEMENTS

The third step in cognitive restructuring is to create a new list of truthful coping statements to replace your old irrational beliefs about public speaking. Once you have recorded your fears and worries about public speaking and identified them as irrational beliefs including **must thoughts, irrational conclusions,** and **cognitive distortions,** then you are ready for this next step. You will need to develop truthful coping statements to replace each of your ultimate fears.

Exercise 7.3a will help you replace your cognitive distortions and irrational conclusions with positive coping statements. You will check the list of positive coping statements to see which ones apply to your fears.

Exercise 7.3a A List of Positive Coping Statements

As you read through the following coping statements, please place an "x" by the statements that apply to **your** distortions and irrational conclusions about public speaking.

____ 1. *To replace Awfulizing or Microscopic Viewing:* Dreading to give a speech is an unrealistic and extreme exaggeration of the importance that one speech has on my life. Giving a speech occupies such a small amount of time in relationship to my entire life that it could be compared to the smallest star in the sky or a pin dropped on an interstate highway.

____ 2. *To replace I-Can't-Stand-It-Itus:* Since I am able to speak without nervousness in many situations involving my friends or family, I can learn to speak without nervousness in front of any fellow earthlings and to enjoy the experience.

OR

I have coped with hard tasks or other difficulties in my life so I can cope with the challenge of public speaking. In fact, I am committed to meeting this challenge.

____ 3. *To replace Damnation Thinking or Microscopic Viewing about your audience:* My audience is not evaluating or judging my every word or every hair on my head. Fellow earthlings want the best for me and like myself, are simply looking for helpful ideas that can enrich their lives. I can be acceptable and worth listening to without being perfect.

____ 4. *To replace Always-and-Never Thinking:* Life is full of trials and errors, successes, and setbacks. No matter what my experience has been in the past, I can overcome my fear of public speaking. I can become an adequate and confident public speaker.

____ 5. *To replace Peephole Thinking:* I will direct my attention to presenting the ideas in my speech. Focusing on my fears or feelings of nervousness will only prevent me from concentrating on my speech.

____ 6. *To replace Ignoring the Positive or Damnation Thinking:* Blaming myself for past shortcomings or failures will not foster my goals. I can focus on successful experiences in my life and learn positive coping statements to replace my must thoughts.

____ 7. *To replace Microscopic Viewing:* Public speaking is a communication encounter, not a magnified performance. My goal is to clearly communicate my message. I can use the same conversational communication style I use daily with family and friends. I can be myself.

____ 8. *To replace Emotional Reasoning or Labeling:* Feelings of activation when I give a speech are normal and to be expected. (Only those in a coffin no longer experience stress.) Such feelings are a sign that I am alive and enthused. They are not a sign that I have lost control.

OR

Even if I feel some anxiety, I will not focus on it. I will act as if I am not anxious. I will believe in myself and my goals to help others.

___ 9. *To replace All-or-Nothing Categorizing:* It is not a disaster or a calamity to make a mistake, forget a detail, or give a poor speech. I will be satisfied doing the best I can.

OR

If I lose my place in my speech or forget something, my speech is not ruined. My audience friends will wait while I look at my notes and move on to my next point.

___ 10. *To replace Personalizing or Damnation Thinking:* I will not base my opinion of myself on what others think or what they appear to be thinking about me. Some may appreciate my ideas, others may not, but I can appreciate my effort. Everyone has a right to express their opinion, and I have a right to respectfully share my ideas.

___ 11. *To replace Psychic Reading:* Thinking I am going to do poorly or worrying about a speech will only agitate and demoralize me. I cannot predict the future. I have no need to worry about my speech because I will contribute something by planning, researching, and sharing my ideas.

___ 12. *To replace Labeling:* Everyone experiences some degree of anxiety or nervousness when communicating in front of others. Feeling a bit of anxiety or nervousness is not bad. It does not mean I am weird, and it will not keep me from reaching my goals.

___ 13. *To replace Phonyizing:* I will gracefully accept any positive comments and praise from others about my speech or myself. I will just say, "thank you," when I am complimented. I can accentuate the positive in my life and appreciate my achievements.

___ 14. *To replace Perfectionizing:* No one is perfect or fully competent in all aspects of life. I do not have to look perfect or be perfect in this world or give a perfect speech. I will try to contribute my part. I will unconditionally accept myself.

OR

Other persons who are not better than myself have given speeches and will continue to give speeches. I can be myself in front of others. I can provide ideas that will be helpful to some.

(These coping statements are loosely based on rationalities suggested by Simpson (1982).

Developing Your Own Coping Statements. Now is the time to systematically rebuild your thoughts. You will write down a coping statement to replace *each* of your irrational fears. You may refer to the list of coping statements in the last section or create your own or combine any on the list. It is important that they are *your* coping statements (i.e., personal and useful to you). They should fit your list of ultimate fears, distortions, and irrational conclusions about public speaking. Please follow the directions in Exercise 7.3b.

Exercise 7.3b Your Coping Statements List

Please complete the following chart in order to develop your own coping statements list about public speaking. Transfer your Ultimate Fears List from Exercise 7.1 to this chart. Label the distortion or irrational conclusion (see Exercises 7.2b and 7.2c) in each item on your fears list. (Some of your thoughts could involve several distortions, but just label them as you see fit.) Then write your own coping statement for each fearful thought (see Exercise 7.3a). Try to make each coping statement personal and useful to you. DO NOT SKIP THIS EXERCISE. IT IS AN ESSENTIAL STEP IN CONQUERING YOUR FEAR OF PUBLIC SPEAKING. (For an example, see Kim's COPING STATEMENTS LIST on pages 69–70.)

ULTIMATE FEARS: Irrational Beliefs, Worrisome Thoughts, Negative Self-Talk	IRRATIONAL CONCLUSION OR DISTORTION AND WHY IT IS NOT TRUE	POSITIVE COPING STATEMENTS
1.	1.	1.
2.	2.	2.
3.	3.	3.
4.	4.	4.
5.	5.	5.

(over)

Ultimate Fears: Irrational Beliefs, Worrisome Thoughts, Negative Self-Talk	Irrational Conclusion or distortion and Why It Is Not True	Positive Coping Statements
6	6	6
7.	7.	7.
8.	8.	8.
9.	9.	9.
10.	10.	10.

EXAMPLE: KIM'S COPING STATEMENTS LIST

ULTIMATE FEARS: Irrational Beliefs and Negative Self-Talk	IRRATIONAL CONCLUSION OR DISTORTION AND WHY IT IS NOT TRUE	POSITIVE COPING STATEMENTS
1. I worry I will make a mistake. My speech will be ruined. I will get embarrassed and look really stupid.	1. Damnation Thinking and All-or-Nothing Categorizing and Perfectionizing. I do not have to be perfect to be acceptable. Others who are not better than myself have given speeches.	1. If I lose my place in my speech, forget something, or make a mistake, my speech is not ruined. My audience friends will wait while I look at at my notes and move on to my next point.
2. Everyone will be watching everything I do and say—and I can't stand it.	2. I-Can't-Stand-It-Itus and Damnation Thinking=Everyone is NOT judging my every word. They are NOT hypercritical toward me or my speech.	2. Fellow Earthlings in my audience want the best for me and are like myself, they are simply looking for ideas to aid or enrich their lives.
3. I'll look like a fool when I try to perform in a formal way. It will be terrible.	3. Awfulizing and Microscopic Viewing=Public speaking is a communication encounter, like speaking with family or friends whom I respect.	3. Giving a speech is not a magnified performance. It is communicating my ideas with others. I can be myself. I can use my everyday basic conversational skills.
4. People will see me blush and shake or hear my voice crack. They will laugh and think poorly of me.	4. Damnation Thinking and Perfectionizing=Most people will not even notice the nervousness I feel. They will focus on the ideas I share.	4. No one is perfect or fully competent in everything. I do not have to look perfect or be perfect. I will contribute what I can, and it will help some people.
5. Since once I forgot important points, I worry I will go blank or forget something again.	5. Always-and-Never Reading= The past does not predict the future. I will prepare and use my notes.	5. Life is full of trials and errors, successes and setbacks. No matter what my experience has been, I can become an adequate and confident public speaker.
6. Feeling nervous is awful, therefore pubic speaking is awful. I should feel calm in order to become a good speaker. I shouldn't feel nervous.	6. Awfulizing and Labeling= A little nervous activation is normal before delivering a speech. I do not have to focus on it. I can let it energize me.	6. Everyone experiences some degree of nervousness when presenting in public. Feeling nervous is not bad. It will not keep me from fulfilling my goals.

(continued on page 70)

EXAMPLE: KIM'S COPING STATEMENTS LIST (continued)

ULTIMATE FEARS: Irrational Beliefs and Negative Self-Talk	IRRATIONAL CONCLUSION OR DISTORTION AND WHY IT IS NOT TRUE	POSITIVE COPING STATEMENTS
7. The audience will think my speech is boring and uninteresting.	7. Damnation Thinking and Psychic Reading=I cannot predict what my audience will think. Some will like it and others won't care.	7. Worrying about a speech or how others will rate me will only agitate and demoralize me. I have no need to worry. I will plan and contribute something by sharing my ideas.
8. I will speak so fast that no one will be able to understand me.	8. Always-and-Never Thinking and Psychic Reading=I cannot predict the future. I will try to communicate so everyone can understand and hear me.	8. I will direct my attention to presenting the ideas in my speech. I will not focus on my fears or feelings of nervousness. If I sense I am speaking too fast, I will slow down a bit.
9. If I feel nervous, I could lose control or I could hyperventilate.	9. Emotional Reasoning= Feelings of nervousness will not predict what will happen.	9. Feelings of activation are normal and to be expected. They are a sign I am alive and enthused. They are not a sign I have lost control.
10. Someone will ask a question I can't answer. Then I will feel and look stupid.	10. Damnation Thinking and Personalizing and All-or-Nothing Categorizing=It is not bad to say you don't know the answer or to suggest sources to find the answer.	10. I will NOT base my opinion of myself on what others think. It is NOT a disaster to give a poor speech or not be able to answer a question. I will be satisfied doing the best I can.
11. I just can't stand public speaking. I don't know what to say or do when it comes to speaking in public.	11. I-Can't-Stand-It-Itus and Damnation Thinking=I can learn public speaking skills in a public speaking class.	11. Since I am able to speak without nervousness in front of my friends or family, I can learn to speak without nervousness in front of any fellow earthlings.

7.4 STEP FOUR: PRACTICING YOUR COPING STATEMENTS

The fourth step in cognitive restructuring is to memorize and practice your coping statements so you will have a new script in your mind to replace your old irrational beliefs. Start by trying to ***memorize at least three*** of your coping statements. When your old must thoughts, irrational conclusions, or distortions automatically pop into your mind, then you will be ready to challenge them with new coping statements.

You should try to *read through your personal list of coping statements every day* or until you know it by heart. Try to read it aloud so you feel a connection with each of your coping statements. You may want to post your coping statements list on a mirror where you dress, on a refrigerator, or other conspicuous place where you can be reminded to read your list often. You may want to share your list of coping statements with a trusted friend who also is anxious about public speaking.

Every time you feel anxious, nervous, or fearful about public speaking, you should ask yourself: "What am I thinking that caused me to feel this way?" Then, look for the must thought, irrational conclusion, or cognitive distortion you were thinking. Identify it as an irrational belief. Then repeat your coping statement to replace the belief.

Lastly, you should try to set small weekly goals for speaking out in class or in meetings or giving short speeches so you can practice using your coping statements. Before long they will almost automatically replace your old thoughts. *Don't be discouraged if your old irrational beliefs keep popping into your mind. You have been thinking those thoughts for a long time. It will take a few weeks of diligent practice to disconnect those automatic must thoughts.* So be heartened and know that your efforts will be rewarded with practice.

If you faithfully practice these four steps in cognitive restructuring you will notice that your fear and nervousness about public speaking will drastically diminish over the next few weeks:

1. Create (write out) a list of all worrisome thoughts, negative self-talk, and fears about public speaking (i.e., make an "Ultimate Fears List").
2. Identify and label the must thoughts, irrational conclusions, and cognitive distortions on your list so that you know they are irrational beliefs—lies or twisted truths that you will no longer believe.
3. Develop a new list of truthful coping statements to replace your must thoughts, irrational conclusions, and distortions. Your coping statements should be personal and useful to you.
4. Practice and memorize your coping statements. Every time you catch yourself feeling anxious, fearful, or nervous about public speaking, look for your negative self-talk, cognitive distortions, and irrational conclusions. Immediately confront those thoughts and replace them with your positive coping statements. Work at believing your coping statements more than your irrational beliefs. Set small weekly goals for speaking up in a small group or giving a speech, where you can practice using your coping statements.

❄ ❄ ❄

Kim, age 31, wrote "When I first practiced the coping statements they sounded silly. As I began to put them in my own words, I was amazed at how much they helped me. . . . It took a few weeks to stop awfulizing and damnation thinking and to keep the coping statements in my mind. But the more I kept practicing them, the more they took hold. My fear about public speaking went down with every week I practiced them. Cognitive restructuring works, if you use it and practice.

❊ ❊ ❊

CHAPTER SUMMARY

Cognitive restructuring is a cognitive technique based on the premise that if you change your fearful thoughts, you will change the way you feel. Speechfright is an irrational fear because there is no potential danger in the public speaking event. The ABCDs remind us that it is your B=Beliefs (irrational beliefs) about the A=Activating Event (public speaking) that causes your C=Consequences (fear, anxiety, and nervousness), not the event itself. Cognitive restructuring involves D=Disconnecting the irrational beliefs about public speaking in order to eliminate the C=Consequences. Irrational beliefs include "must thoughts," which are the perfectionistic demands you make on yourself, others, and the situation. Must thoughts lead to irrational conclusions (i.e., awfulizing, I-can't-stand-it-itus, damnation thinking, always-and-never thinking) and cognitive distortions (peephole thinking, ignoring the positive, psychic reading, microscopic viewing, emotional reasoning, all-or-nothing categorizing, labeling, personalizing, phonyizing, and perfectionizing). By discovering your irrational beliefs about public speaking, identifying your distortions and irrational conclusions, and then learning new positive coping statements to replace them, your fear, anxiety, and nervousness associated with public speaking will greatly diminish with practice.

REVIEW QUESTIONS

After reading this chapter, you should be able to answer the following questions:

1. Explain the premise of cognitive restructuring and which personality dimension it targets.
2. Briefly describe the four steps in the cognitive restructuring technique.
3. Compare and contrast rational beliefs versus irrational beliefs. Give an example for each type.
4. Explain the ABCDs of irrational fear.
5. What are "must thoughts," and what do they have to do with speechfright?
6. Compare and contrast the communication perspective versus the performance perspective. Which perspective represents a rational belief?
7. Describe the four irrational conclusions and what impact they have on speechfright.
8. Briefly describe the ten cognitive distortions about public speaking.
9. Identify three coping statements that are most helpful for you.
10. Explain how to replace your old script of irrational beliefs with the new positive coping statements so that the coping statements become more automatic than your old irrational beliefs.

CHAPTER EIGHT

SYSTEMATIC DESENSITIZATION

The systematic desensitization technique (Wolpe, 1958) targets the affect, sensation, and imagery personality dimensions. It is specifically designed to reduce the excessive physical activation and the tense feelings of nervousness associated with fear or anxiety (McCroskey, Ralph, & Barrick, 1970). The goal of systematic desensitization is to help you develop a new relaxation response to a feared or anxiety-provoking event, such as public speaking. By using this technique you will learn to replace nervous feelings and excessive physical sensations (i.e., a pounding or rapid heartbeat, indigestion, nausea, sweating, dry mouth, trembling hands and feet, blushing, etc.) with feelings of calmness.

Systematic desensitization (SD) is based on learning theory. From educational psychology, you may have heard of the term "stimulus-response." Ivan Pavlov, for example, is known for training his dogs to salivate (response) upon hearing a bell ring (stimulus). He did this by systematically bringing food to his dogs at the same time as he rang a bell. The dogs learned to associate the ringing of a bell with food. Soon they salivated, even without the food, as a response to the stimulus of the ringing bell. In a similar way, you are going to train your body to respond to the stimulus (a public speaking event) with a relaxation response to replace the fear response.

Systematic Desensitization (SD) involves these steps:

1. Create a hierarchy of fearful events (instances or steps toward the feared event that are arranged in order of intensity).
2. Train your body in progressive and deep muscle relaxation until your body knows how to completely relax. (It is important for your body to be able to differentiate between relaxation and tension).
3. Condition your body to relax in response to all the events on your hierarchy. (You will create a new stimulus-response bond of relaxation to public speaking as you systematically practice relaxation in response to each of the stimulus events you bring to mind in mental pictures [visualizations].)

In the past you may have learned (or unknowingly trained yourself) to associate fear and nervous sensations with public speaking. In order to break this stimulus-response bond between public speaking and fear, you will need to learn a new calming, relaxation response to public speaking. Through SD you will train yourself to associate relaxation with public speaking and thus create a new stimulus-response bond (like Pavlov trained his dogs to salivate when a bell rang). The result will be a significant reduction in the excessive physical sensations and feelings you experience toward public speaking.

8.1 STEP ONE: CREATE A HIERARCHY OF FEARED EVENTS

The first step in learning SD is to create a sequential list of fearful events that lead to anxiety about public speaking (e.g., reading a book on public speaking, receiving a public speaking assignment, writing a speech outline, practicing a speech, waiting to give a speech, etc.). You should try to identify specific situations during the speech-making process that arouse your fear or anxiety. After listing these situations, you can rank them on a 100-point scale to determine if your list does range from the least anxiety-provoking to the most anxiety-provoking instance.

The hierarchy of fearful events should include between ten and fifteen feared situations (Friedrich & Goss, 1984). If it consists of less than ten, the event has not been broken down enough to use the desensitization process (i.e., the situations will be too intense). If the hierarchy consists of too many events (twenty or more), the technique will take you too long to learn (Booth-Butterfield & Booth-Butterfield, 1992).

You should try to create your own list of feared events in public speaking. However, many people who fear public speaking report a similar hierarchy of feared events. Consequently, there are lists of feared events that have worked well to help others overcome public speaking anxiety (Friedrich & Goss, 1984; McCroskey, 1972; Paul, 1966). Exercise 8.1a includes a sample list of feared events you can use or one that can guide you in creating your own list.

The communication research on the SD technique shows that your list does NOT have to be a perfect hierarchy (i.e., an exact hierarchy of your fears) in order for the technique to be used successfully (Yates, 1975). What is important is that you have a practical hierarchy to work from that systematically breaks down your fear into ten to fifteen situations of feared events. If the sample list presented in Exercise 8.1a includes most of your feared situations, you want to use this list. If you have other feared situations in the speechmaking process, you can add them to the sample list and develop your own hierarchy of feared events. Please follow the directions in Exercise 8.1b.

Exercise 8.1a A Hierarchy of Feared Events in Public Speaking

Please place an "x" by each event on this list that stimulates any fear, anxiety, or nervousness for you.

___ 1. Thinking about speech class while sitting in your room alone.

___ 2. Sitting in speech class or in a situation where you will be assigned to give a speech.

___ 3. Reading a textbook about the speech-making process.

___ 4. Hearing about a formal speaking assignment.

___ 5. Preparing your speech by writing your speech outline.

___ 6. Rehearsing your speech alone in your room (or in front of a friend).

___ 7. Getting dressed the morning of the speech.

___ 8. Walking to the room and entering it on the day of your speech.

___ 9. Waiting to give your speech, while another person speaks.

___ 10. Walking up before your audience.

___ 11. Presenting your speech before the audience (and seeing the faces looking at you).

___ 12. Walking back to your seat after delivering your speech.

Exercise 8.1b Your Hierarchy of Feared Events in Public Speaking

Creating a hierarchy of feared events is the first step in the learning the SD technique. You will identify specific situations during the speech-making process that arouse your fear or anxiety. In the space provided, record at least ten feared situations in public speaking. You will want to refer to the "Hierarchy of Feared Events in Public Speaking" list in Exercise 8.1a (you can use the items on that list or add and delete items from the list). After listing these situations, go back and rank each instance on a 100-point scale from *1=least anxiety-producing event* to *100=most anxiety-producing event* in order to determine the order for your hierarchy (e.g. 20 points=Reading a textbook about the speech-making process; 50 points=Hearing about a formal speaking assignment; 100 points=Presenting a speech before an audience).

RANK POINTS (FROM 1 TO 100)	FEARED INSTANCE IN SPEECH MAKING
1.	
2.	
3.	
4.	
5.	
6.	
7.	
8.	
9.	
10.	
11.	
12.	
13.	
14.	
15.	

8.2 STEP TWO: TRAIN YOUR BODY IN PROGRESSIVE MUSCLE RELAXATION

The second step is the heart of the SD technique. It involves training your body to completely relax using an audiotape of prerecorded deep muscle relaxation instructions. SD will be effective for you only if you take time to learn deep muscle relaxation and practice it before moving on to the third step. It is essential that your body be able to differentiate between relaxation and tension, as well as be able to maintain deep relaxation.

SD is not hypnosis; it will not bring on a dreamlike state. You will be conscious and in control at all times. In fact, you should try not to fall asleep. However, if you do fall asleep the first time you try to relax, don't give up; keep trying to stay awake while you train your body to relax. (Busy students occasionally fall asleep the first time they try to teach their bodies to relax because they have deprived themselves of relaxation and sleep in the rigors of college life.) In order to avoid falling asleep, try to practice the relaxation step when you are not overly exhausted and while sitting up in a chair. If you lay down in a horizontal position, you will probably doze off and not be able to train your body.

The SD technique uses Jacobson's (1938) progressive muscle relaxation training to teach your body to relax. Progressive muscle relaxation involves systematically tensing and holding muscle groups for about five to ten seconds, and then relaxing them for another ten to fifteen seconds while mentally focusing on how good relaxation feels (Friedrich & Goss, 1984). Usually each muscle group is tensed and relaxed at least twice before moving on to the next set of muscles The following muscle groups are *successively tensed and then relaxed*:

1. hands (clench);
2. biceps and triceps (bend hands upward at wrist, pointing fingers, flex biceps);
3. shoulders (shrug shoulders);
4. neck (push head against chair, then forward);
5. mouth (press lips tightly);
6. tongue (extend, retract);
7. tongue (press to roof and floor of mouth);
8. eyes and forehead (close eyes tightly, wrinkle forehead);
9. breathing (inhale, hold, exhale);
10. back (arch);
11. midsection (tighten muscles including buttocks);
12. thighs (tighten muscles);
13. stomach (suck in stomach);
14. calves and feet (stretch out both legs);
15. toes (point toes upward and downward).

The easiest way to train your body in progressive muscle relaxation is to use an audiotape. You can use the audiotape "Conquering Speechfright" that is designed to accompany this handbook (see order form in back of book), or you can create your own audiotape using the script presented in Exercise 8.2. You should practice deep muscle relaxation with an audiotape at least a few times, so your body is trained in what it means to fully relax, before moving to the third step of SD.

To prepare to learn deep muscle relaxation, you must take your audiotape and tape player to a room where it is quiet and free of distractions and other people. (Do not try to practice SD while driving a car, as deep relaxation will interfere with driving and can cause an accident.) You will want to sit upright in a chair, with both feet on the floor. You may want to support your head on a headrest or lean it against a wall. (Do not lay down.) Remove your glasses. Allow your arms to rest comfortably on your thighs or the arms of a chair. Now, turn on your audiotape of progressive (and deep) muscle relaxation exercises.

Exercise 8.2 Script for Learning Progressive Muscle Relaxation

You can use the prerecorded "Conquering Speechfright" audiotape (see order form on back page) or create your own tape. To create your own, use a tape recorder and a new ninety-minute audiocassette tape (forty-five minutes per side). Try to speak in a calm and relaxed voice. Follow this script. (The time in parentheses is meant as a guide to tell you how long to pause before continuing. Do not speak the time aloud.)

With your eyes closed, take three deep abdominal breaths. Inhale deeply (pause five seconds). Exhale slowly through the mouth. Take another deep breath, hold it (pause five seconds). Now exhale slowly. Again, inhale deeply and hold it (pause five seconds). Exhale slowly and completely. Begin to concentrate on letting go of all tension.

Now, try to concentrate on each part of your body. Beginning with your left hand, tightly clench your left fist. Hold your muscles very tightly, but not so tight that it is uncomfortable. Study the tension in your left hand and forearm. Note how strained these muscles feel (pause five seconds).

Now relax your left hand. Let it relax very comfortably on your lap or on the arm of your chair. Note how pleasant relaxation feels and how it contrasts with the tension (pause ten seconds).

Again tightly clench your left fist. Hold your muscles very tightly. Study the tension and hold it (pause five seconds).

Relax your hand. Let your left hand open and get very relaxed. Notice the pleasant feeling of relaxation in your left hand and how it contrasts with the tension (pause ten seconds).

Now with your right hand, tightly clench your fist. Study the tension in your right hand and in your forearm. Note how strained the muscles feel (pause five seconds).

Now relax. Let your right hand open up so that even your fingers feel relaxed (pause ten seconds).

Again, clench your right fist. Your muscles feel tense, but not painful. Study the tension in your hand (pause five seconds). Now relax your right hand. Open up the fingers on your right hand. Note how relaxation feels (pause ten seconds).

Now with your left hand resting on your lap or arm of a chair, bend your hand backward at the wrist, toward your shoulders so that your fingers are pointing to your face. Study the tension in your hand and forearm (pause five seconds).

Relax those muscles. Notice how pleasant relaxation feels in contrast to tenseness (pause ten seconds).

Again with your left hand, point your fingers backward and toward your shoulders. You should feel the tension in the back of your hand. Study the tension (pause five seconds).

Relax your hand once again on your lap or chair. Notice how pleasant relaxation feels (pause ten seconds).

Now with your right hand resting on your lap or arm of a chair, bend it at the wrist, pointing it backward toward your shoulders. Study the tension in the back of your hand and forearm (pause five seconds)

Let your hand fully relax on your lap or chair. Notice the difference between tension and relaxation (pause ten seconds).

Again, bend your right hand at the wrist and point it backward toward your shoulders. Study the tension and hold it (pause five seconds).

Relax the right hand. Let it go loose and limp. Note the feelings of relaxation (pause ten seconds).

Now with both arms, tense your biceps by bringing your forearms toward your shoulders and making a muscle with both arms. Study the tension in your forearms (pause five seconds).

Relax. Drop your arms to your chair or your thighs and note how pleasant it feels to release the tension (pause ten seconds).

Again tense your biceps by bringing your forearms up toward your shoulders and making a muscle with both arms. Feel the tension (pause five seconds).

Relax. Drop your arms back to your lap or chair. Note how very pleasant it feels to release the tension (pause ten seconds).

Next, shrug both shoulders. Tighten your shoulders by raising them up as if you are going to touch your ears. Note the tension in your shoulders, in your neck, and in your back. Study the tension (pause five seconds).

Relax your shoulder muscles. Note how relaxed you feel (pause ten seconds).

Shrug your shoulders again. Raise them way up and feel the tension in your shoulders and neck and back (pause five seconds).

Relax them again and notice how very pleasant it feels to release the tension (pause ten seconds).

Tense your muscles in your forehead by raising your eyebrows as much as you can. Study the tension around your eyes and above your eyes and forehead (pause five seconds).

Smooth out your forehead muscles. They are feeling relaxed (pause ten seconds).

Now again, tense the muscles in your forehead by raising your eyebrows as much as you can. Study those tensions (pause five seconds).

Relax the forehead muscles. Smooth them out. Notice how very pleasant it feels to release the tension and enjoy the relaxation (pause ten seconds).

Next, tense the muscles around your eyes by closing your eyes very tightly. Study the tension (pause five seconds).

Relax. Your eyes remain lightly closed and relaxed (pause ten seconds).

Again, clench your eyelids very tightly. Hold it (pause five seconds).

Relax those muscles around your eyes. Notice how pleasant it feels to release the tension around your eyes (pause ten seconds).

Now press your tongue firmly into the roof of your mouth. Tighten all those muscles in your mouth and hold it (pause five seconds).

Let your tongue drop in your mouth to a very relaxed position. Notice how relaxed your mouth and tongue feel (pause ten seconds).

Again, press your tongue firmly into the roof of your mouth. Study the tension (pause five seconds).

Relax those muscles that control your tongue (pause ten seconds).

Next press your lips together. Study the tension around your mouth (pause five seconds).

Relax the muscles around your mouth. Note how pleasant it feels to relax the mouth (pause ten seconds).

Again press your lips together. Study the tension (pause five seconds).

Relax those muscles. Your lips will come apart slightly (pause ten seconds).

Next, tighten the muscles in the back of your neck, pushing your head back as far as you can against the chair or until you can feel tension on your neck. Study the tension in your neck (pause five seconds).

Relax and let your head come forward to a resting position. Feel that relaxation flowing into your entire neck area and throat (pause ten seconds).

Again, push your head back against the chair. Study the tension in the back of your neck (pause five seconds).

Relax those neck muscles. Feel the relaxation flowing into your neck as your head comes forward to the resting position (pause ten seconds).

Now bring your chin forward as if to bury it in your chest. Study the tension in the front of the neck (pause five seconds).

Relax by returning your head to its resting position. Notice how pleasant relaxation feels as tension is released (pause ten seconds).

Again, bring your chin forward until it is almost buried in your chest. Study the tension in the front of your neck (pause five seconds).

Relax. Notice how pleasant it feels to relax (pause ten seconds).

Next, arch your back. Stick out your chest and lift your back off of your chair. Study the tension in your back (pause five seconds).

Relax. Notice the contrast between the tension and the comfortable feeling of relaxation (pause ten seconds).

Again, arch your back, way back, lifting your back off the chair. Study the tension (pause five seconds).

Relax. You feel all tension leaving your body and relaxation spreading to every muscle (pause ten seconds).

Tighten the muscles in your chest by taking a very deep breath. Hold it and study the tension in your chest (pause five seconds).

Exhale and relax (pause ten seconds).

Again, take a deep breath so that your abdomen rises instead of your chest. Hold it and study the tension (pause five seconds).

Exhale and relax (pause ten seconds).

Now, take a deep breath in through your nose and tighten your stomach as tight as you can and hold it (pause five seconds).

Relax your stomach. Note the difference between tension and the feelings of relaxation (pause ten seconds).

Tense your stomach muscles one more time. Breathe in through your nose and tighten your stomach as much as you can. Hold it as tight as you can and study the tension (pause five seconds).

Relax your stomach muscles. Feel the relaxation spreading into your stomach area. Your breathing has returned to normal (pause ten seconds).

Now tense your buttocks by pushing them into the seat of your chair. Feel the tension. Hold that position (pause five seconds).

Relax those muscles. Notice the contrast between tension and relaxation (pause ten seconds).

Again, push your seat into your chair. Study the tension and hold it (pause five seconds).

Relax those muscles (pause ten seconds).

Now squeeze the thigh muscles in both of your legs by straightening both legs and lifting your feet off the floor. Study the tension in your thigh muscles and hold it (pause five seconds).

Relax and let your feet drop (pause ten seconds).

Again, squeeze your thigh muscles. Straighten both legs and stretch them out as far as you can (pause five seconds).

Relax your thighs (pause ten seconds).

Next, bend your feet and toes up toward the ceiling, tensing the muscles in the calves and ankles. Hold it (pause five seconds).

Relax. Let the muscles in your calves get very loose and relaxed (pause ten seconds).

Again, tense your calf muscles by bending your feet upward toward the ceiling. Notice how strained the muscles feel (pause five seconds).

Let go and relax. Feel the relaxation coming into your calf muscles (pause ten seconds).

Curl the toes of both feet under and tense your arch area so you can feel the tension in the arch of your foot. Study that tension (pause five seconds).

Relax. Notice how pleasant relaxation feels in contrast to the tension (pause ten seconds).

Again, curl the toes of both feet under. Study the tension in your feet and in your arches (pause five seconds).

Relax and enjoy the calmness (pause ten seconds).

Now go back through several muscle groups that you have been relaxing. When each muscle group is mentioned, make sure it is relaxed.

Relax both hands (pause ten seconds).

Relax your forearms and upper arms (pause ten seconds).

Relax your shoulders and neck (pause ten seconds).

Relax your forehead and facial muscles (pause ten seconds).

Relax your mouth (pause ten seconds).

Feel the relaxation spreading from your head and neck to your chest and stomach (pause ten seconds).

Relaxation is spreading to your buttocks (pause ten seconds). Relax your thighs (pause ten seconds).

Relax your calves and feet (pause ten seconds).

You have just completed the deep muscle relaxation phase in SD. Slowly open your eyes, and then shut the tape off.

You should continue to practice with your audiotape until your body is very familiar with relaxation. You want your body to be able to relax on demand, so it will take a few days of practice to train your body to quickly bring your muscles to a feeling of deep relaxation.

8.3 STEP THREE: CONDITION RELAXATION BY ADDING MENTAL PICTURES FROM THE HIERARCHY

The third step in the SD technique is to condition your body to relax in response to all the events listed on your hierarchy. To condition relaxation in your body, you will create mental pictures (visualizations) of each of the situations listed on your hierarchy while at the same time maintaining deep muscle relaxation. In other words, you will create a new stimulus-response bond (public speaking with relaxation) as you systematically practice relaxation in response to each of the stimulus situations you bring to mind. The new stimulus-response bond (public speaking–relaxation) will replace the old stimulus-response bond (public speaking–fear/anxiety/excessive physical sensations). For this step, you can follow the explanation in the following pages or continue to use the "Conquering Speechfright" audiotape that is available with this book.

You may wonder how bringing pictures (visualizations) to mind while you are completely relaxed can condition your body to respond with relaxation later in the real situations of speech making. One explanation is that your body only knows what is happening by what your mind is thinking (Booth-Butterfield & Booth-Butterfield, 1992). If you are completely relaxed when your mind sees public speaking, your body has no other way of getting information to the contrary. Consequently, your body is tricked into learning a relaxation response to the situation you have imagined. The relaxation will be superimposed over the anxiety response, which in turn will weaken. This principle is called **"reciprocal inhibition"** (Wolpe, 1958; Friedrich & Goss, 1984)

Another explanation of why SD works is called **"habituation"** (Watts, 1979). Habituation means that as you repeatedly practice a new response to a stimulus, the former response decreases in effect. Therefore, the more you practice SD and visualize the anxiety-provoking situations, the more the old response of anxiety will just go away. You will have conditioned yourself away from the anxiety.

To add the third step of SD, you must be completely relaxed. You should practice progressive muscle relaxation until every muscle in your body is relaxed. At the point of deep relaxation and immediately after you have listened to your relaxation audiotape, you will begin to add the first four mental pictures from your hierarchy. But before you begin with your least anxiety-provoking situation, you should call to mind a neutral or non-anxiety-provoking situation in order to practice visualizing mental pictures. The best way to start is by visualizing yourself lying in bed just before falling asleep (you should try to mentally picture the details in your bedroom with you in the bed feeling completely relaxed).

Once you are relaxed and have practiced picturing yourself in an anxiety-neutral situation, you are ready to add the first four mental pictures from your hierarchy of feared events. For example:

1. thinking about speech class while sitting in your room alone;
2. sitting in speech class or in a class where you will be assigned to give a speech;

3. reading a textbook about the speechmaking process; and
4. hearing about a formal speaking assignment.

You should try to hold the mental picture of each situation for a period of fifteen to thirty seconds while maintaining complete relaxation. If any muscle becomes tense, clear your mind of the mental picture and concentrate on relaxing that muscle. When all muscles are relaxed, return to the same mental picture and again try to maintain complete relaxation for fifteen to thirty seconds. Do not move on to visualizing the next situation until you can maintain complete relaxation with the previous situation on your hierarchy.

Once you have visualized all of the first four least-provoking situations from your hierarchy of feared events, take a few deep breaths, open your eyes, and become acquainted with your surroundings again. You should work on adding only four mental pictures at a time in order to give your mind and body a chance to bond relaxation with the mental pictures.

For your next SD practice session, again listen to the relaxation tape. Check to see if you can maintain relaxation with the first four mental pictures. If you can, move on to visualizing each of the next four situations from your hierarchy of feared events. For example:

5. preparing your speech by writing your speech outline;
6. rehearsing your speech alone in your room (or in front of a friend);
7. rising and getting dressed on the morning of the speech; and
8. walking to the room and entering it on the day of your speech.

Again, when you can maintain complete relaxation for fifteen to thirty seconds with each situation, take a few deep breaths, open your eyes, and become acquainted with your surroundings.

At your next session, again listen to the relaxation tape. Check to see if you can maintain relaxation with the previous four mental pictures. If you can, move on to visualizing each of the final four situations from your hierarchy of feared events. For example:

9. waiting to give your speech, while another person speaks;
10. walking up before your audience;
11. presenting your speech before the audience and seeing the faces looking at you; and
12. walking back to your seat filled with energy and confidence.

The situation "presenting your speech before the audience" may take some practice before you can hold the visualization and maintain relaxation for fifteen to thirty seconds. Don't become concerned if you can't hold the visualization and maintain relaxation at first. It will take practice to create the new response bond with the final events listed on your hierarchy. Remember when you feel tension in any muscle, clear your mind of that mental picture and concentrate on relaxing the muscle. When you are completely relaxed, return to the mental picture.

You should try to practice the SD exercise, maintaining deep muscle relaxation while going through all three sets of mental pictures several times. **You will notice benefits after you have practiced SD five to six times.** It is important that you maintain deep muscle relaxation for each of the mental pictures in order to form the new relaxation bond to public speaking. Only move on to the next set of mental pictures after you have maintained deep muscle relaxation with each mental picture in the previous set. When you have maintained relaxation while visualizing all the events listed on your hierarchy, you are ready to try public speaking. As you set small goals for yourself, and practice speaking in public, you may discover new anxiety-provoking situations you want to overcome and can add to your hierarchy list.

If you faithfully practice these three steps in systematic desensitization, you will notice that your excessive physical sensations (activation) and feelings of nervousness associated with public speaking will diminish over the next few weeks:

1. Create a hierarchy of fearful events in public speaking (or steps toward the feared event that are arranged in order of intensity).
2. Train your body in progressive and deep muscle relaxation until your body knows how to completely relax and can differentiate between relaxation and tension.
3. Condition your body to relax in response to all the events on your hierarchy. (You will mentally picture each of the events on your hierarchy while maintaining deep muscle relaxation. Visualize only four events at a session so that your body has a chance to create the new stimulus-response bond with each event.)

Keep practicing SD and you will acquire new relaxed feelings associated with public speaking.

❄ ❄ ❄

Gina, age 25, wrote "I used to feel physically out of control when giving a speech. My body felt like it shook on the inside and outside. Even my voice would shake. My stomach would be in knots. I didn't believe anything could help. But SD did. I practiced SD five or six times. . . . I noticed a big difference by my next speech. My body felt under control. . . . SD worked for me and I know it will help anyone who really uses it.

❄ ❄ ❄

CHAPTER SUMMARY

Systematic desensitization (SD) targets your affect, sensation, and imagery personality dimensions. It is based on learning theory. In the past you learned (unknowingly trained yourself) to associate a fear response (nervousness and excessive physical activation) with the stimulus (public speaking). In order to break your old stimulus-response bond, you can train your body using SD to associate relaxation with public speaking, forming a new stimulus-response bond. How SD works can be explained by the principles of "reciprocal inhibition" or "habituation." SD involves creating a hierarchy of feared events (instances) in public speaking, training your body in progressive muscle relaxation, and visualizing each of the events in your hierarchy while maintaining deep muscle relaxation. When you have maintained relaxation while visualizing all the events listed on your hierarchy, your excessive physical sensations and feelings of nervous activation associated with public speaking will noticeably diminish.

REVIEW QUESTIONS

After reading this chapter, you should be able to answer the following questions:

1. Which personality dimensions does systematic desensitization (SD) target?
2. What is the goal of SD?
3. Briefly explain the three steps in systematic desensitization.
4. Describe how to create a hierarchy of feared events.
5. What is progressive muscle relaxation?
6. How can you train your body in deep muscle relaxation?
7. Explain the principles of "reciprocal inhibition" and "habituation" and how each relates to using SD for overcoming speechfright.
8. How many feared events should you visualize at each practice session?
9. How often should you practice SD before you notice results?
10. What results can be attained from practicing SD?

CHAPTER NINE

Mental Rehearsal (Visualization)

Mental rehearsal, also called "visualization," targets your imagery and cognitive personality dimensions. This technique involves mentally rehearsing an event before participating in it and has been used by many successful athletes to help them attain peak performance. Mental rehearsal prepares your mind and body for the event and thereby alleviates some of the situational causes of anxiety (novelty, conspicuousness). In speech making, this technique is practiced just before you give a speech and with a particular speech in mind.

9.1 THE COGNITIVE PSYCHOLOGY OF POSITIVE MENTAL IMAGERY

Mental rehearsal, according to cognitive psychologists, is based on the premise that we hold images in our mind of what we perceive as future situations. If the image is negative, then we will feel anxiety (Fanning, 1988). On the other hand, if the image of future situations is positive, then we will have positive feelings and our anxiety will be limited. Consequently, one way to counter feelings of anxiety is to learn to associate positive images with a future event, such as public speaking.

Mental rehearsal stresses the development of positive thinking and positive images. It will increase your concentration and help you think positively about an upcoming speech. It will help you feel confident and positive instead of negative and anxious.

9.2 MENTAL IMAGERY AND ATHLETIC SUCCESS

Mental rehearsal was first developed by Roberto Assagioli in the 1970s and has been used extensively by athletes and trainers since that time (Assagioli, 1976; Anthony, Maddox, & Wheatley, 1988; Garfield, 1984, 1986). You have probably watched the Olympics or another athletic event in which skiers, gymnasts, runners, or skaters were seated with eyes closed and were methodically moving their bodies from side to side. Most athletes are trained to mentally picture themselves running, skating, skiing, or performing their event confidently and successfully before the competition begins.

Mental rehearsal is a complementary technique to behavioral practice. Athletes rely on mental rehearsal as a final preparation before the race or game, but it cannot and should not

Harcourt Brace & Company

ever replace training or practice. It will prepare your mind for a positive and successful experience. The C. W. Post college basketball team study is one classic example that shows the impact of mental rehearsal on performance (Brydon & Scott, 1994). The basketball players, in an effort to improve free-throw shooting, were divided into three groups. The groups were assigned to: 1) practice free-throw shooting, 2) practice free-throw shooting and mental rehearsal, and 3) practice mental rehearsal only. The group that showed the most improvement over time was Group 2, who practiced the combination of mental rehearsal and behavioral rehearsal.

9.3 MENTAL REHEARSAL AND SPEECH ANXIETY

In the mid-1980s, college professors Joe Ayers and Tim Hopf (1985) began to use the visualization technique to help students decrease their anxiety levels in public speaking classes. Several studies have shown that the technique is very helpful at reducing anxiety when students mentally rehearse a very positive and successful speaking experience prior to giving a formal speech in class (Ayers & Hopf, 1989).

The easiest way to learn mental rehearsal is to practice the technique using an audiotape designed to help you see yourself in a positive light while giving a speech. An audiotape of a mental rehearsal for a classroom speech is on the "Conquering Speechfright" audiotape that accompanies this book, or you can create your own audiotape from the script in Exercise 9.3. It will take about ten minutes per practice session and another ten to fifteen minutes to record the audiotape. When you play the audiotape, try to go to a room where it is quiet and you can be undisturbed. Do not try to practice mental rehearsal while driving a car.

Exercise 9.3 Sample Script for the Mental Rehearsal Technique

Use a tape recorder and try to speak in a calm and relaxed voice in order to make your own tape. Follow this script, which is based on a visualization script suggested by Ayers and Hopf (1989). (The time in parentheses is meant as a guide to tell you how long to pause before continuing. Do not speak the time aloud.)

Try to become as comfortable as possible in your chair. Position your hands on your lap or on the arms of the chair so they feel relaxed. Remove your glasses, if you like, in order to get more comfortable. Close your eyes. Move around until you feel comfortable.

Take a deep abdominal breath so that your abdomen rises, not your chest. Hold it. (Pause five seconds.) Now slowly release it.

Take another deep abdominal breath. Hold it. (Pause five seconds.) Slowly release it. Note how good you feel while you are breathing deeply. Feel the relaxation starting to flow through the limbs of your body to your fingers and toes. Take one more deep, comfortable breath. Hold it for a few seconds. (Pause five seconds.) Slowly release it. Now return to your normal breathing pattern. Again, try to get as comfortable as you can in your chair.

Begin to mentally picture the dawn of the day on which you are going to give your speech. Try to picture the day just as it will be when you arise. You have had a very restful night. See yourself getting out of bed in the morning. You feel energized and confident. You say to yourself, "I am prepared to meet the challenges of this day; I am looking forward to sharing my ideas with my friends or classmates." (Pause five seconds.)

See yourself taking out of your closet the clothes that you think are right for your plans for the day and will help you feel good about yourself. As you are dressing, notice that you have a very positive attitude. You say, "I believe in myself and my goals to help others." (Pause five seconds.)

Try to picture any activities you usually do before you leave for class. (Pause five seconds.) Next, see yourself driving or riding or biking or walking to the classroom where you will be giving your presentation. See yourself smiling as you practice the deep abdominal breathing exercises on the way. Note how self-assured you feel. You have worked hard to prepare and rehearse your speech. You have practiced your positive coping statements. (Pause five seconds.)

See yourself walking into the building and then into the room where you will speak. Your classmates appear warm and friendly. They greet you with very positive remarks. A friend nearby tells you that you'll do a great job today. Another friend says she's been looking forward to hearing your speech. (Pause five seconds.)

You feel thoroughly prepared to speak to your class as you walk over to your seat. You are mentally and physically ready for the occasion. You have thoroughly researched your topic and any related issues. Your outline is complete. Because of your rehearsing, you are confident about the timing. You are prepared in every way for what you are presenting today. You are calm, yet ready. You say to yourself: "I appreciate my efforts; I know I can provide ideas that will be helpful to some." (Pause five seconds.)

See yourself sitting at your seat in the classroom. You are conversing very comfortably and confidently with those around you. You assure others that you are looking forward to hearing from them. You feel absolutely confident about your presentation and your ability to deliver your speech in a lively and assured manner. You know your message will be beneficial to many in your audience. (Pause five seconds.)

It is now approaching your time to speak. As you wait, see yourself taking a relaxed abdominal breath and saying: "My audience wants me to succeed. I will do the best I can to offer the ideas I have prepared." (Pause five seconds.)

Next, see yourself moving to the front of the room. You are feeling very positive about your presentation. You may have visual aids tucked under your arm and you are confident they will enhance your presentation. You are well-organized and well-planned and ready to go. (Pause five seconds.)

Visualize yourself delivering your presentation. You're really quite good. You notice that your audience is giving you positive feedback with head nods, eye contact, and smiles. They are conveying the message: they're with you, and they're interested in what you are saying. You are helping them. (Pause five seconds.)

Your attention-getter and opening remarks go the way you have planned. You establish your credibility and preview your points. You move smoothly into the body of your speech. Your first main point comes forth just as you had planned. The evidence that you use—examples, statistics, and quotations—are well-chosen and help make your points. You can see that you have your audience's attention and interest. (Pause five seconds.)

See yourself unfolding each of your main points smoothly. Your language is fluent, and the words come easily as in everyday conversation. You are passionate and use gestures and vocal inflections to emphasize your points. Now, see yourself finishing the body of your speech and moving to the ending. You summarize the main points, and the entire conclusion is a fitting finale to everything you have spoken.

When you've finished your last few words, you say to yourself: "This presentation went very well. I am pleased with myself and my speech. The introduction drew my audience into the topic. My main points were clear and easy to follow. My evidence was convincing. My conclusion was an appealing and fitting end to my entire speech. I used vocal inflections to convey my enthusiasm and commitment. I paused effectively to emphasize important ideas. I even used gestures and body movements to complement my verbal message."

See yourself receiving applause and praise from your audience. People are expressing their appreciation. A few raise their hands to ask questions, which you confidently answer—or you make suggestions where they could go for additional information. (Pause five seconds.)

You are relaxed and gratified. You accomplished your goal of sharing your ideas with others. You've done a good job and you feel it. You are energized and ready for the rest of your day. Giving a presentation has been a truly fulfilling and confidence-building experience for you. You can look forward to other new challenges.

Begin to return your thoughts to this time and this place. Take a deep abdominal breath. Hold it. (Pause five seconds.) Let it go. Again, take a really deep abdominal breath. Hold it. (Pause five seconds.) Exhale. Do this a few more times. (Pause five seconds.) Get ready to open your eyes. Take as much time as you need to transition back to this time and place. Now open your eyes. You are ready to go!

9.4 MENTAL REHEARSAL AND THE DAY OF YOUR SPEECH

Mental rehearsal works best when you practice it right before you give a speech with that particular speech in mind. It is best to practice this technique the evening before, as well as on the day you will give your speech.

After you have practiced mental rehearsal with the audiotape, you will be able to recreate the mental imagery without using the tape. This will make the technique very handy to use during a busy day when you can find just a few minutes to sit back and visualize your presentation.

On the day you will be giving your speech, try to keep only positive thoughts about your speech in mind. Try to visualize the people in your audience and their attitude toward you as very positive. Mentally rehearse each of your main points, as well as the introduction and conclusion.

❊ ❊ ❊

Sam, age 19, said "I used to picture myself saying something stupid when speaking in front of any group. I could just see everyone laughing at me. . . . I learned a visualization technique as part of a sports program in high school. I never thought of using something similar for public speaking. . . . Mentally picturing myself doing a good job giving a speech has helped me feel more confident and at ease. I feel more prepared. . . . I will always use visualization to prepare for a speech."

❊ ❊ ❊

9.5 MENTAL REHEARSAL AND BEHAVIORAL PRACTICE ARE BOTH IMPORTANT

Mental rehearsal is very important, but it should never take the place of the thorough preparation essential for a successful speech. Mental rehearsal works best when it is used along with behaviorally rehearsing your speech. (Remember the basketball team that mentally and behaviorally rehearsed free throws was the most successful.) Investigating your topic (researching), carefully outlining your speech, and thoroughly practicing your delivery will make you feel more comfortable and increase your confidence level.

Behavioral practice means you practice your delivery with an outline on note cards several times before you deliver your speech. It involves practicing your speech aloud before a mirror or wall and then practicing it before a few supportive friends or family members. Many students have reported that the amount of time they spent planning an outline and practicing their delivery is in direct correlation with how much security and confidence they feel when they deliver the speech.

If you plan and behaviorally practice your speech and then practice the mental rehearsal technique to visually rehearse a positive presentation, you will make a giant step toward becoming a confident speaker. You will be able to manage your fear and anxiety.

CHAPTER SUMMARY

Mental rehearsal targets the imagery and cognitive personality dimensions. It is based on the premise that we all hold images about future situations. If the image is positive, we have positive feelings; if the image is negative, we feel anxiety. Mental rehearsal stresses the development of positive thinking and positive images. The technique has been used extensively by athletes to attain peak performance and by public speakers to reduce anxiety. At first, you should use an audio tape to rehearse a positive and successful speaking experience. Later, you can develop your own visualizations of a particular public speaking event. Mental rehearsal works best when you practice it right before you give a speech and with a particular speech it mind. It should never take the place of thorough preparation and behavioral practice. It was designed to complement behavioral rehearsal and prepare your mind for a positive experience.

REVIEW QUESTIONS

After reading this chapter, you should be able to answer the following questions:

1. Which personality dimensions does mental rehearsal target?
2. On what premise from cognitive psychology is mental rehearsal based?
3. Explain why mental rehearsal should never replace preparation and behavioral practice.
4. Describe how to practice mental rehearsal.
5. When is the best time to practice mental rehearsal?
6. Explain the meaning of behavioral practice and how it complements mental rehearsal.

CHAPTER TEN

Physical Exercise, Interpersonal Support, and Skills Training

Physical exercise targets the drugs/biological personality dimension and is an established way to reduce stress and anxiety in our lives in general. In addition, it helps reduce anxiety for public speakers when practiced directly before a presentation. Interpersonal support targets the interpersonal relationships personality dimension and helps buffer the impact stress has on our lives, helps us experience commonality, and helps us stay committed to our goals. Skills training targets the behavior personality dimension and is essential for developing confidence and competence in public speaking, as well as reducing anxiety from perceived lack of skills.

10.1 PHYSICAL EXERCISE REDUCES STRESS AND PUBLIC SPEAKING ANXIETY

Physical exercise has been shown to benefit a person physiologically, emotionally, cognitively, and even socially (Sachs, 1982). Researchers have found significant improvement in the anxiety, fear, and stress levels of people who started exercise programs (Otto, 1990; Sachs, 1982; Sedlock & Duda, 1995). Exercisers are better able to manage stress than nonexercisers (Stone, 1987). In fact, psychologists report, "Vigorous exercise is the natural outlet for the body when it is in the 'fight or flight' state of arousal" (Davis et al., 1988, p. 225).

Some researchers have tested the influence of physical exercise on the stress related to public speaking—directly before a person delivers a speech (Otto, 1990; Schwartz & Kaloupek, 1987; Sedlock & Duda, 1994). Just ten minutes of vigorous bicycle pedaling, for example, prior to delivering a speech had a positive effect on the speakers (Otto, 1990). They reported less physiological sensations (e.g., sweating, trembling, nervous stomach, tightness, lumps in the throat, and rapid heart beating), less disfluencies (e.g., uhs, uhms), and less negative moods than the speakers who did not exercise before speaking.

One recent study found significant relationships between the frequency, intensity, and duration of an exercise program and less public speaking anxiety (Carr, 1996). In other words, people who exercised often, with intensity (days worked out to a point of

Harcourt Brace & Company

perspiration or breathlessness), and for a longer period of time reported less anxiety or fear about giving a speech in general. (The average workout frequency was 3.5 days per week; the average intensity level [times per week of workout to perspiration or breathlessness] was 2.75 days; and the average duration of a workout was about 49 minutes [Carr, 1996].) In addition, increased workout intensity correlated with decreased anxiety in group discussion, meetings and overall CA; increased duration correlated with decreased meeting anxiety and overall CA; increased frequency correlated with decreased anxiety in meetings and overall CA (Carr, 1996).

Since moderate exercise prior to giving a speech, as well as a general exercise program, help reduce the reported anxiety and stress levels for those giving a speech, you may want to include exercise in your speechfright reduction plan. The Surgeon General and the United States Department of Health and Human Services, as well as most medical and health organizations, recommend a regular exercise program to maintain optimal health (U.S. Department of Health and Human Services, 1991). This handbook does not advocate a particular exercise program as treatment for public speaking anxiety, but does present this information for your consideration. You should always consult your physician before starting any exercise program.

This book does point out that exercise can be helpful in reducing stress and anxiety prior to giving a speech. Consequently, if your dorm or university parking lot location presents you with a ten- to twenty-minute brisk walk to a campus building, consider it therapeutic, especially on days you will be giving a speech.

Many athletes have an exercise routine they do before a big game or event. The exercise serves to warm up the muscles but also helps reduce pregame nervousness or anxiety. For example, no one mentions how funny those football players look doing exercises on the field before kickoff. We all know they are doing warm-up exercises. In the same way, public speakers can have a warm-up routine to reduce anxiety and get the blood flowing into the limbs. The windmill is an exercise that combines the deep abdominal breathing exercise from Chapter Six with arm movements. It's one exercise that college students in public speaking classes have used as part of their warm-up routines prior to delivering graded speeches.

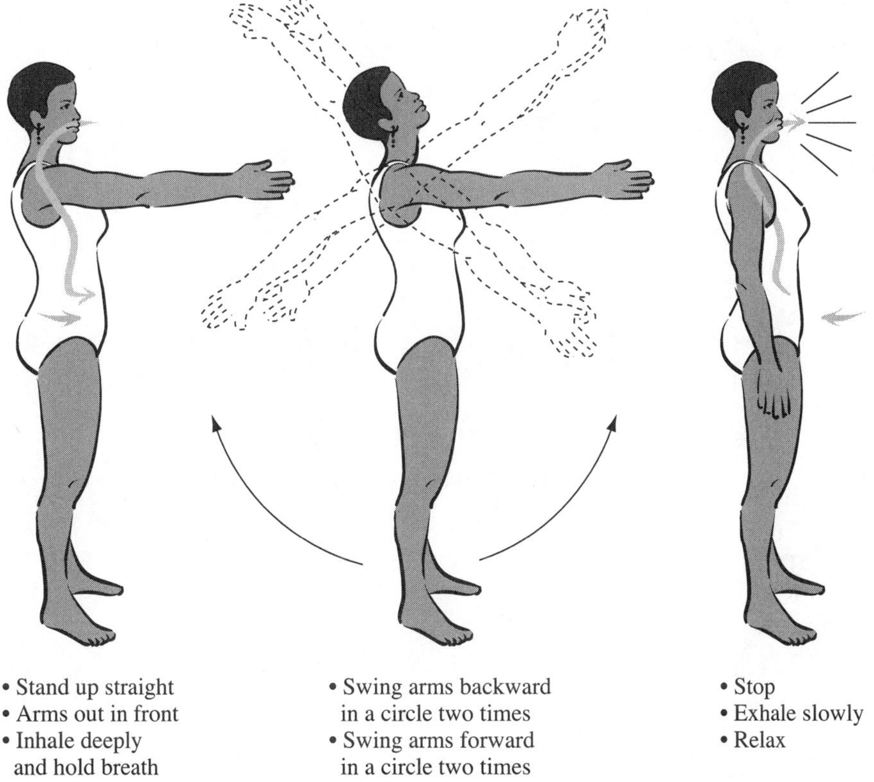

The Windmill Warm-up Exercise

Exercise 10.1 The Windmill Warm-up Exercise

The "Windmill Warm-up" combines physical activity with deep breathing. Just like athletes who exercise before a game to warm up and relieve stress, you too can use physical exercise and deep breathing to relieve stress before a speech. Following these steps:

1. Stand up straight, with shoulders thrown back and head reaching to the ceiling.
2. Place your arms out in front of you.
3. Inhale deeply and hold your breath.
4. Now, swing both arms backward in a circle two times and then swing them forward in a circle two times.
5. Stop and exhale slowly and fully until all of your air is exhaled.
6. Then, tell your body go limp and to RELAX.

Repeat the Windmill Warm-up exercise several times, especially when you have been sitting at a desk or riding in a car for a long time. It will help reduce tension before delivering a speech, warm up your muscles, and get the blood flowing to your fingertips (to reduce cold hands, generated by the fight or flight response).

10.2 INTERPERSONAL SUPPORT BUILDS CONFIDENCE AND REDUCES STRESS

Interpersonal support, also called social support or mutual support, means having others in our lives who can share similar struggles, similar emotions, and similar thoughts (Jacobs, Harvill, & Masson, 1988). Several studies have reported that social support helps us manage stress in general, buffers its impact on our lives, and helps us stay committed to our goals as we feel a commonality and sense of belonging (Daniels & Guppy, 1994; Overholser, Norman, & Miller, 1990; Ray & Miller, 1994).

Interpersonal support for overcoming speechfright is best discovered in a group where people are working toward the same goals and can be mutually supportive of one another. A beginning public speaking class or a class designed for students with excessive fear of public speaking is a good place to find people who have the same goals as yourself. Such classes can help you feel that you are not alone in your attempt to become a confident speaker. In addition, they will provide you with a supportive environment and a safe arena to practice public speaking skills. Many students have reported that the encouragement they received from others in a public speaking class is what built their confidence and enabled them to learn more skills.

If you do not have the support of a special class designed to help students overcome speechfright, then you should try to find a supportive friend with whom you could share your goals and progress, but don't share your struggle to overcome speechfright with a judgmental family member or friend who has no interest in public speaking. You cannot expect that person to be supportive when you practice a technique or speech.

10.3 SKILLS TRAINING BUILDS SKILLS AND REDUCES FEAR

Skills training (Fremouw & Zitter, 1978; Fawcett & Miller, 1975) targets the behavior personality dimension and is designed to help people learn and practice the skills necessary for effective public speaking. It is based on the idea that people fear public speaking because they lack the skills or think they lack the skills. Obviously, everyone can become anxious or fearful about doing something new when they don't know how to do it. The goal of this technique is to train people in public speaking skills as one way to reduce the fear of public speaking. The skills training technique follows the skills deficit model (Phillips, 1991), which assumes people avoid communication because of perceived lack of skills. It's the perceived lack of skills that produces the anxiety and negative consequences in communication situations, which in turn causes more anxiety and further avoidance. In other words, the more you believe you lack the skills, the more anxiety you experience, and the more you avoid situations where you could learn the skills. In order to break the anxiety-avoidance chain, you can enroll in a workshop or class where you can learn public speaking skills. Communication research indicates that skills training works best in combination with other techniques (Allen, Hunter, & Donohue, 1989; Ayers & Hopf, 1993; Dwyer, 1995; Rossi & Seiler, 1989; Whitworth & Cochran, 1996) and when other techniques are taught first (Ayers & Hopf, 1993). Consequently, if you previously tried to learn public speaking skills, but retreated because of your anxiety, you probably needed to learn other anxiety-reduction techniques first before attempting to learn public speaking skills.

This book does not teach skills training in public speaking because speaking skills are best acquired through taking a public speaking class. Such a course will teach you how to research, organize, and deliver informative, as well as persuasive, speeches. Some of the specific skills you will learn in a public speaking course include:

1. choosing a topic,
2. selecting a specific purpose and central idea,
3. analyzing the audience and situation,
4. researching the topic,
5. organizing and outlining the ideas,
6. incorporating supporting material,
7. creating introductions and conclusions,
8. preparing note cards and visual aids,
9. rehearsing and delivering a speech.

Skills training is most effective when it narrowly targets specific behaviors for improvement (Richmond & McCroskey, 1995). So you will want to enroll in a class where you can focus on developing specific skills, one or two at a time. Effective skills training involves the following components:

1. identifying a skill deficiency;
2. observing models of the skilled behavior;
3. setting attainable goals;
4. acquiring knowledge about the new skills;
5. visualizing the new skills;
6. practicing the new skills in a nonthreatening environment, as well as in a natural environment; and
7. self-monitoring your progress (Glaser, 1981; Kelly, 1989; Richmond & McCroskey, 1995).

You can look for classes or workshops that are designed especially to help individuals overcome speechfright. Begin by asking a college advisor about the availability of the programs. Such classes could help you target specific behaviors in skills training, as well as help you learn the other techniques. If an overcoming speechfright class is not available, choose a basic public speaking class that encourages you to set modest and specific goals with each speaking opportunity. For example, a first assignment might be a short one- or two-minute mini-speech on a familiar topic in which you can practice specific behaviors before moving on to longer speaking opportunities.

As you acquire public speaking skills in concert with applying the other techniques presented in this handbook, you will significantly reduce your anxiety, fear, and nervousness about public speaking. You will become a confident and effective speaker.

Exercise 10.3 Public Speaking Skills Assessment

Learning public speaking skills is an important step in overcoming speechfright, as well becoming an effective and confident speaker. Please read though the following list of basic public speaking skills and place an (x) by the skills you need to learn in a public speaking course in order to become a confident and effective speaker.

___ 1. Choosing your topic

___ 2. Selecting a specific purpose and central idea for your speech

___ 3. Analyzing your audience and the situation

___ 4. Researching the topic and using the library

___ 5. Organizing and outlining your ideas

___ 6. Incorporating supporting material into your speech

___ 7. Creating introductions and conclusions

___ 8. Preparing note cards and visual aids

___ 9. Rehearsing and delivering your speech

CHAPTER SUMMARY

Physical exercise targets the drugs/biological personality dimension and helps reduce stress and anxiety in general. It also specifically reduces anxiety for public speakers when practiced directly before a presentation. Interpersonal support targets the interpersonal relationships personality dimension and helps reduce stress in general and buffers its impact on our lives. In addition, mutual support helps us stay committed to our goals and experience a sense of commonality and belonging that is important when developing any new skill or overcoming any challenge. Skills training targets the behavior personality dimension and is essential for developing confidence and effectiveness as a public speaker, as well as reducing speechfright from perceived lack of skills. Try to choose a basic public speaking class that encourages you to set modest and specific goals with each speaking opportunity.

REVIEW QUESTIONS

After reading this chapter, you should be able to answer the following questions:

1. Which personality dimension does physical exercise target?
2. Explain how physical exercise helps reduce speechfright.
3. Which personality dimension does interpersonal support target?
4. Explain how interpersonal support can help a person overcome speechfright.
5. Where can you expect to find interpersonal support for overcoming speechfright?
6. Which personality dimension does skills training target?
7. Where can you learn the skills training technique?
8. What do you plan to do to increase your public speaking skills in the next month? In the next year?

Part 3

Developing a Personal Plan for Conquering Speechfright

CHAPTER ELEVEN

A MULTIDIMENSIONAL APPROACH

This chapter will help you apply the techniques you have just learned in a personalized program. A combinational and multidimensional approach to treating speechfright has been presented in Chapter Five of this handbook. As you might recall, the **combinational approach** is based on communication research that shows the greatest reduction in public speaking anxiety is achieved when a combination of techniques are used, instead of only a single treatment (Allen, Hunter, & Donohue, 1989; Ayers & Hopf, 1993; Dwyer, 1995a; Dwyer, 1995b; Rossi & Seiler, 1989; Whitworth & Cochran, 1996). The **multidimensional approach** is based on the multimodal counseling model (Lazarus, 1989) that emphasizes the importance of matching treatment techniques to each of seven human personality dimensions. Since you know it is important to use a combination of techniques, this chapter will show you how to match specific techniques to your personality dimensions so you can determine which combination of techniques will be most useful to *you*.

11.1 THE BASIC DIMENSIONS OF PERSONALITY AFFECTED BY ANXIETY

Like all human beings, each of us has seven dimensions that make up our personalities (Lazarus, 1989). Since we are "biological beings who move, feel, sense, imagine, think, and relate to one another, each of these dimensions requires our attention when problems emerge" (Lazarus, 1978, p. 8). Consequently, treatment for speechfright, like any other problem that affects our emotions, can best be addressed from a multidimensional perspective.

As you will remember from Chapter Five, the acronym "BASIC ID" describes the seven interactive personality dimensions that should be considered in any multidimensional evaluation process:

B= BEHAVIOR (overt behaviors, acts, habits, reactions that can observed and measured);

A= AFFECT (emotions, moods, and strong feelings);

S= SENSATION (bodily sensations, such as pain, tension, discomfort, or nausea and the touching, tasting, smelling, seeing, and hearing of our five senses);

Harcourt Brace & Company

I= IMAGERY (vivid scenes, pictures, or images that come to mind including the way you see yourself in particular situations);

C= COGNITION (thoughts, attitudes, ideas, beliefs, or opinions);

I= INTERPERSONAL RELATIONSHIPS (interactions with significant others);

D= DRUGS or BIOLOGICAL FUNCTIONS (general physical well-being, amount of stress in your life, use of drugs, and exercise programs you follow) (Lazarus, 1989).

This BASIC ID will function as an educational guide to help you analyze your own speechfright and self-select the most appropriate treatment techniques (O'Keefe, 1985).

When multidimensional assessment is applied to the fear of public speaking, it can help you determine which technique you should begin using as well as which combination of techniques will be most useful to you. The first step in multidimensional assessment is to assess *your* personality dimensions involved in *your* speechfright. To do this, please complete Exercise 11.1.

Exercise 11.1 Assessing Your BASIC ID Personality Dimensions

Please answer the questions below in order to assess speechfright in each of your personality dimensions. You may notice some or all of these dimensions involved in your speechfright:

1. **BEHAVIOR** refers to observable acts, habits, or behaviors. In regard to your speechfright, list the behaviors in a public speaking situation you would like to learn, change, decrease, or increase. (E.g., I want to learn to write a speech outline, develop delivery skills, fulfill the time requirement, and decrease disorganization and use of "uhms.")

2. **AFFECT** refers to emotions, moods, and strong feelings. In regard to your speechfright, list the emotions or strong feelings you experience while preparing or delivering a speech. (E.g., I experience overwhelming fear, nervousness, and feelings of impending doom or failure.)

3. **SENSATION** refers to physical sensations (i.e., pain, tension, discomfort, nausea) and the touching, tasting, smelling, seeing, and hearing of our five senses. In regard to your speechfright, list the negative bodily sensations that you experience before, during, or immediately after you give a public presentation. (E.g., I feel stomach butterflies, blushing, rapid or pounding heartbeat, sweating, dry mouth, shivering, nausea, or lightheadedness.)

4. **IMAGERY** refers to vivid scenes, pictures, or images that come to mind, including the way you see yourself. In regard to your speechfright, describe the negative ways you "picture yourself" and your surroundings when you imagine delivering a speech. (E.g., I imagine my entire audience laughing or snickering at me. I see myself overwhelmed with fear or passed out on the floor.)

5. **COGNITION** refers to your thoughts, attitudes, ideas, beliefs, or opinions. In regard to your speechfright, describe your negative thoughts and condemning self-talk about giving a speech. (E.g., I cannot meet the audience's demands—they expect me to give a perfect speech; I know I will make a mistake, sound stupid, or look like a fool.)

6. **INTERPERSONAL RELATIONSHIPS** refers to your interactions withsignificant others. In regard to your speechfright, describe any negative ways others treat you when you have given a speech or any concerns you have about the others when learning public speaking skills. (E.g., My English teacher said I was incompetent because I gave a speech and didn't fulfill the time requirement. My roommate laughs at me when I practice a speech.)

7. **DRUGS OR BIOLOGICAL FUNCTIONS** refers to your general physical well-being, amount of stress in your life, use of drugs, and any exercise or health programs you follow. (E.g., I am always stressed because of work, school, and family. I seldom exercise or get enough sleep. I have no stress reduction plan.)

Now that you realize which of your personality dimensions are involved in your speechfright, you are ready to discover which dimension initiates your speechfright by "tracking the firing order."

11.2 TRACKING THE FIRING ORDER: GETTING TO THE ROOT OF YOUR FEAR

There is a way of determining which technique might be most helpful to you in the beginning. It is called "tracking the firing order" (Lazarus, 1989). Tracking (or determining) the firing order means to pinpoint the personality dimension where your speechfright begins (fires) and the sequence of dimensions involved in your speechfright.

Determining firing order is important because it helps get at the root of your speechfright. Once you know the root of your speechfright, you can choose the techniques most fitted to the origination of your fear. Treating speechfright at its root or initiating point in your personality will result in the most permanent change and reduction of anxiety.

Determining the best technique for treating your CA does not diminish the importance of learning all the techniques. Tracking the firing order can be compared to playing a game of dominos. If you can stop the first domino from falling, the remaining dominos will have a greater chance of staying upright or there will be less impact on them. Your goal in tracking the firing order is to locate the first domino (dimension where your speechfright begins) and then to keep it from falling. If you can determine where your speechfright starts and then treat that dimension with one of the techniques, you can stop the chain reaction and lessen the effects CA has on your other personality dimensions. See the following two examples.

❄ ❄ ❄

Sarah, age 21, said: "I suddenly **feel** my heart pound and my face turn bright red before it's my turn to give a speech. Then I **think,** "Oh, this is terrible; I've lost control—people will notice how nervous I am. I **picture** myself passed out on the floor with everyone staring at me and then **fear** overwhelms me."

❄ ❄ ❄

In Sarah's situation, speechfright begins in the sensation dimension (i.e., she physically feels her heart pound and her face turn bright red). The firing order (sequence of dimensions involved in Sarah's speechfright) is 1) sensation (she physically feels), 2) cognition (she thinks), 3) imagery (she imagines), 4) affect (she emotionally feels). The technique most effective for managing Sarah's speechfright will be the one targeted to the source of the problem—the **SENSATION DIMENSION**

❄ ❄ ❄

John, age 24, said: "I always **think** that people will laugh at my ideas and I will sound stupid. Then I **imagine** people staring at me while I say something stupid or stand frozen—forgetting my entire train of thought. Next, I **feel** my heart pound, my stomach turn, and my mouth get dry. **Fear** overcomes me.

❄ ❄ ❄

In John's situation, speechfright begins in the cognition dimension (i.e., he thinks people will laugh at him and he will sound stupid). The firing order (sequence of dimensions involved in John's speechfright) is 1) cognition (he thinks), 2) imagery (he imagines),

3) sensation (he physically feels), 4) affect (he emotionally feels). The technique most effective for managing John's speechfright will be the one targeted to the source of the problem—the **COGNITION DIMENSION.**

Your goal is to find the top dimension in your firing order so that you can *begin* by applying a treatment technique to it. In addition, you will want to look for the sequence of dimensions involved in your speechfright so you can choose techniques that fit those dimensions and form a program tailored to your personality. In the next exercise, you will track the firing order of dimensions involved in your speechfright.

Exercise 11.2 Tracking Your Firing Order

In order to track your firing order, you will need to determine which dimension of your personality initiates your speechfright.

1. Imagine your instructor, employer, or boss has just told you that you must give a speech to twenty-five people within the next hour. With that scenario in mind, try to analyze where your speechfright begins. Try to rank order the dimensions that fire in your speechfright. Give special attention to ranking the top three dimensions.

RANK
(1–7)

___ a. Do you immediately ***think***: "Having to give a speech would be awful. I can't do it! I would make a fool of myself." If irrational, negative, or unproductive thoughts are the first to fire, the top of your firing order is **COGNITION.**

___ b. Do you immediately ***feel (physically)*** any of the following sensations (even before a thought enters your mind): nausea or stomach tightness, heart racing, heart palpitations, blushing, sweating, light-headedness or other physiological reactions? If bodily sensations are the first to fire, the top of your firing order is **SENSATION.**

___ c. Do you immediately and vividly ***visualize*** yourself in a scene where you faint in front of the audience, are the focus of audience laughter or jeers, run out of the room, or are engaged in any other negative activity? If negative mental pictures are the first to fire, the top of your firing order is **IMAGERY.**

___ d. Do you immediately ***feel (emotionally)*** upset, fearful, anxious, or nervous? If emotional feelings of fear or anxiety are the first to fire, the top of your firing order is **AFFECT.**

___ e. Do you immediately react with avoidant **behaviors**, such as procrastination or running from the situation? Do you avoid public speaking because you have **no skills?** If avoidant behaviors related to lack of public speaking skills are the first to fire, then the top of your firing order is **BEHAVIOR**.

___ f. Do you feel over-stressed in general so that giving a speech just adds one more stressful situation to your already **stressful life-style** in which you get very little exercise, are overworked, take drugs or alcohol to cope, and/or eat poorly? If stress in general, use of drugs, and/or poor physical well-being are the first to fire, the top of your firing order is **DRUGS OR BIOLOGICAL FUNCTIONS.**

___ g. Do you immediately wish you had friends to call or a support group to encourage you to learn public speaking skills? If a desire for a support group (i.e., mutually supportive friends) fires first, the top of your firing order is **INTERPERSONAL RELATIONSHIPS.**

2. Which dimension is at the top of your firing order (ranked #1)?

3. List the firing order of the top three dimensions involved in your speechfright (ranked #1, #2, #3).

11.3 MATCHING TREATMENT TO PERSONALITY DIMENSIONS

Once you know the firing order of the dimensions involved in your speechfright, you can easily decide which technique to begin using. The following list of techniques and the personality dimension that each technique targets will help you select the technique that matches the top of your firing order:

1. **Cognitive Restructuring targets the *Cognitive dimension.*** If Cognition is at the top of your firing order, begin using Cognitive Restructuring.
2. **Systematic Desensitization targets the *Affect, Sensation,* and *Imagery dimensions*.** If Affect, Sensation, or Imagery is at the top of your firing order, begin using Systematic Desensitization.
3. **Mental Rehearsal (Visualization) targets the *Imagery* and *Cognitive dimensions.*** If imagery or cognition is at the top of your firing order, concentrate on using mental rehearsal.
4. **Deep Abdominal Breathing targets the *Affect* and the *Sensation dimensions.*** If Affect or Sensation is at the top of your firing order, begin using Deep Abdominal Breathing (it is an important part of Systematic Desensitization and Mental Rehearsal, too).
5. **Physical Exercise and Stress Reduction Routines targets the *Drugs/Biological Functions dimension.*** If Drugs/Biological Functions is at the top of your firing order, contact your physician and work with a professional on developing a stress-reduction program for your life and a more healthy lifestyle.
6. **Interpersonal Support targets the *Interpersonal Relationships dimension.*** If Interpersonal Relationships is at the top of your firing order, try to enroll in a workshop or class designed specifically to help individuals overcome speechfright, or a course that will provide a supportive environment where you can develop supportive friends working on the same public speaking goals.
7. **Skills Training targets the *Behavior dimension*.** If Behavior is at the top of your firing order, you should immediately enroll in a public speaking class or workshop where you can learn and practice public speaking skills. (The class should include delivering speeches and helping you set new goals for each speech.)

In order to match techniques to the dimensions in your firing order, complete Exercise 11.3.

Exercise 11.3 Matching Techniques to Your Personality Dimensions

Once you have assessed your personality dimensions (Exercise 11.1) and tracked your firing order (Exercise 11.2), you are ready to match techniques to the top three dimensions in your firing order. Referring to Exercise 11.2 and using the chart in this exercise, list the top three dimensions in your firing order according to rank. Start with the dimension ranked #1.

RANK	DIMENSION	SPEECHFRIGHT-REDUCTION TECHNIQUE
1.		
2.		
3.		

Referring to the following list of personality dimensions and specific speechfright-reduction techniques targeted to those dimensions, complete the preceding chart with the techniques matched to your top three dimensions.

PERSONALITY DIMENSIONS AND SPEECHFRIGHT-REDUCTION TECHNIQUES

PERSONALITY DIMENSION	SPEECHFRIGHT-REDUCTION TECHNIQUE
Behavior Dimension:	Skills Training (enroll in a public speaking class where you can learn and practice public speaking skills)
Affect Dimension:	Systematic Desensitization and Deep Abdominal Breathing
Sensation Dimension:	Systematic Desensitization and Deep Abdominal Breathing
Imagery Dimension:	Systematic Desensitization and/or Mental Rehearsal (Visualization)
Cognitive Dimension:	Cognitive Restructuring and/or Mental Rehearsal
Interpersonal Relationships:	Interpersonal Support (enroll in a class or workshop where you can receive support from others while you learn to overcome speechfright)
Drugs / Biological Functions:	Physical Exercise Programs and Stress-Reduction Plans (contact your physician to help you start a stress-reduction and physical exercise program)

Now you know what techniques to begin using. Since your goal is to apply a technique to the top of your firing order in order to get at the root of your speechfright, focus on the technique (or techniques) that matches the dimension ranked #1 in your firing order. Next, apply a technique to the dimension ranked #2 in your firing order and then to the one ranked #3.

Matching techniques to personality dimensions in your firing order should not become something so precise that you begin to worry if you truly found the top of your firing order. Tracking the firing order should simply serve as a guide to help you determine which techniques will be most effective for you. Many students report that it helps them understand why one technique works better for one student, while another technique works better for still another student. The techniques that will work best for *you* will fit the dimensions near the top of *your* firing order.

Some students report that what they thought, at first, was the top of the their firing order really turned out be ranked second or third, as they began using the techniques. Others report that it was difficult to choose between two dimensions (which one ranked #1 in the firing order). That, too, is not a problem. Start applying techniques to the top two or three dimensions in your firing order. **Remember, a combinational approach (using at least two or more techniques) works best at overcoming speechfright.** Also keep in mind that your goal is to eventually apply techniques to all of the dimensions involved in your speechfright, which is the multidimensional approach.

When you have applied techniques at every personality dimension involved in your speechfright, beginning with the technique that fits the top of your firing order, you will experience a substantial reduction in your fear, anxiety, and nervousness about public speaking. You will be on the road to becoming a confident speaker.

CHAPTER SUMMARY

The multidimensional approach to overcoming speechfright emphasizes the importance of matching treatment techniques to each of your seven personality dimensions. The acronym BASIC ID serves as an educational guide to help you analyze your seven personality dimensions. Tracking the firing order refers to determining which of the dimension fires first (initiates speechfright). Applying treatment to the top of your firing order is like stopping the top domino (in a game of dominos) from falling. It lessens the impact on the other dimensions and stops speechfright at its initiating point. Speechfright-reduction techniques can be matched to the targeted dimension. Skills training targets the behavior dimension. SD and deep breathing target the affect and sensation dimension. SD and mental rehearsal target the imagery dimension. Cognitive restructuring and mental rehearsal target the cognitive dimension. Interpersonal support targets the interpersonal relationships dimension. Physical exercise and stress-reduction plans target the drugs/biological dimension.

REVIEW QUESTIONS

After reading this chapter, you should be able to answer the following questions:

1. Explain the multidimensional approach to overcoming speechfright.
2. What does the acronym BASIC ID represent?

3. Define "tracking the firing order."
4. What is the purpose of tracking the firing order of dimensions involved in your speechfright?
5. List the seven personality dimensions and the techniques targeted to each dimension.
6. Explain which dimension is at the top of your firing order, how you determined your firing order, and what technique you will use first.

CHAPTER TWELVE

AN ACTION PLAN

Do you feel inspired? You should! Speechfright is *not* an unconquerable monster. You can do it! But remember, in the same way that *passively* watching a videotape on aerobic exercise will not improve your physical well-being, so too *passively* reading this book will not magically make your speechfright disappear. As Chapter One pointed out, you need to:

1. commit yourself to the goal of overcoming speechfright;
2. actively learn the techniques;
3. practice the techniques regularly;
4. participate in public communication so you can put your new knowledge, techniques, and skills to use.

The most important step you can take now is to develop an action plan that includes these measures.

12.1 COMMIT YOURSELF TO YOUR GOAL

The first step in developing an action plan is to make a commitment to your goal. By reading this handbook you are on your way! Make sure you have done all the exercises. Go back and check each of them NOW. If you have skipped any of the exercises, DO THEM NOW.

Read over your answers to Exercises 1.3 and 2.4. Reaffirm your pledge of commitment to overcoming speechfright you made in Exercise 1.3 and reread the goals you recorded in Exercise 2.4. Remind yourself of the commitment you made to those academic, professional, and social goals that overcoming speechfright will help you attain.

As with any other meaningful goal in your life, you will have to make a commitment to channel your time and energy toward reaching your goal. Decide how much time per week you can devote to overcoming your speechfright. For the first few weeks, you will need to set aside one hour every day or at least every other day, for learning and practicing the techniques. Most students find that if they are faithful at practicing the techniques and at setting small goals for speaking in public, they will start to notice at least some change in their anxiety level within a week or two and a major change within a few months.

Harcourt Brace & Company

Conquering speechfright is an achievement that comes in increments. The old adage, "inch by inch everything's a cinch; yard by yard it's rather hard" certainly applies to this goal. Start with a small, faithful, and consistent commitment of time and energy and you will find yourself feeling a little less anxiety with each practice session. With an internal commitment to overcoming speechfright and an external commitment of time and energy, you will make progress.

❊ ❊ ❊

Ana, age 20, said: "I felt a change in my anxiety level after the first week of practicing my coping statements and deep breathing exercises. I really noticed a big change in how I felt after I practiced SD and gave a three-minute mini-speech. I would tell anyone to be committed to practicing the techniques regularly. It took a few months. . . . They changed my life. I no longer fear giving a speech. I never thought I could ever say this, I even enjoy giving a speech."

❊ ❊ ❊

12.2 ACTIVELY LEARN THE TECHNIQUES

By now, you have at least read through the techniques, but have you taken the time to learn the techniques—really *learn* the techniques? Knowing a little bit about the techniques versus having a hands-on working knowledge of them are two different things. Once you have committed yourself to overcoming speechfright, your next step is to actively learn the techniques. Active learning means more than passively reading about something. Active learning means that you ponder what you read and actually write down responses to the exercises. It also means that you record your thoughts about the progress you are making and work with the techniques until you can apply them at a moment's notice.

Working with the techniques involves following the directions and suggestions in order to get the most benefit out of what the techniques were designed to do for you. For example, have you worked with the deep abdominal breathing exercise so you can use it anytime you feel stressful, such as before an exam, job interview, or speech? Have you posted your coping statements list in a conspicuous place where you can read your list often and work at memorizing it? Did you learn to completely relax using deep muscle relaxation, before you added the visualizations? Did you acquire the audiotape that accompanies this handbook, or did you make your own audiotape so you can learn SD and mental rehearsal following an appropriate script? If you have followed these suggestions, as well as the many others explained in each chapter, then you are actively learning the techniques. You will be experiencing change in your anxiety level soon.

12.3 PRACTICE THE TECHNIQUES FOLLOWING A SCHEDULE

The techniques and exercises presented in this handbook will work! They have helped thousands of students reduce excessive fear and anxiety about public speaking. They will help you too, but ONLY IF YOU PRACTICE THEM. The techniques are a vehicle, like a

Exercise 12.3 Developing a Three-Week Practice Schedule

Using the chart below, plan your practice schedule for the next three weeks. When you are finished, record the times in your engagement calendar. Post this schedule where you can see it daily and be reminded of your commitment. (See Kim's example that follows.)

YOUR PRACTICE SCHEDULE:
DATE, TECHNIQUES, AND TIME COMMITMENT IN HOURS

Day and Date	Read Book and Write Exercises	Practice Coping Statements	Practice SD	Practice Breathing Exercises	Practice Mental Rehearsal	Practice Other Stress Reducers
Mon.						
Tues.						
Wed.						
Thur.						
Fri.						
Sat.						
Sun.						
Mon.						
Tues.						
Wed.						
Thur.						
Fri.						
Sat.						
Sun.						
Mon.						
Tues.						
Wed.						
Thur.						
Fri.						
Sat.						
Sun.						

EXAMPLE: KIM'S SCHEDULE
DATE, TECHNIQUES, AND TIME COMMITMENT IN HOURS

Day and Date *February 8–29*	Read Book and Write Exercises	Practice Coping Statements	Practice SD	Practice Breathing Exercises	Practice Mental Rehearsal	Practice Other Stress Reducers
Mon. 8	2 hr.					
Tues. 9	3/4 hr.	1/4 hr.				1/2 hr.
Wed. 10	1/4 hr.	1/4 hr.	1/2 hr.			
Thur. 11	1/4 hr.		1/2 hr.			
Fri. 12						1 hr.
Sat. 13	1/2 hr.	1/8 hr.	1/8 hr.			
Sun. 14			1/8 hr.			
Mon. 15	1/2 hr.					1 hr.
Tues. 16	1/4 hr.		1/8 hr.	1/2 hr.		
Wed. 18				1/2 hr.		
Thur. 19			1/8 hr.	3/4 hr.		1/2 hr.
Fri. 20						1 hr.
Sat. 21			1/8 hr.			
Sun. 22				3/4 hr.		
Mon. 23						1 hr.
Tues. 24			1/8 hr.	1 hr.		
Wed. 25				1 hr.		
Thur. 26						1 hr.
Fri. 27					1/4 hr.	1/2 hr.
Sat. 28						
Sun. 29	1/2 hr.				1/4 hr.	

car that gets you where you want to go but is of little use to you if you leave it parked in the garage. Regularly practicing the techniques will help change your old negative thought patterns, fearful responses, and excessive physical activation into new calm feelings and confident attitudes toward public speaking.

You have lived several years with your old fearful thought patterns and responses, so they will not disappear overnight or because you practiced a technique once or twice. As mentioned in Part 2 of this handbook, you will need to practice the techniques until they become more automatic than your old response patterns. "How long will this take for me?" you ask. For each student, the time will vary. Many students will start to notice a slight change the first week and experience a little more change with each week of practice until over a period of a few months, the new calm response patterns are formed. As always, the students who experience the most change are those who follow a regular practice schedule and are involved in a public speaking class or workshop where they can practice the techniques along with learning public speaking skills and giving short speeches.

The best way to stay on track with practicing the techniques is to develop a practice schedule. This is part of your commitment to overcoming speechfright. Decide on how much time you can spend on practicing the techniques and then schedule your practice sessions on an engagement calendar, just as you would any other important event. Using Exercise 12.3, develop a practice schedule for the next three weeks. Be realistic in scheduling the time you can set aside for practice sessions, and take into consideration your time limitations. Try to set aside about one hour per day or every other day to practice the techniques.

After you have planned and posted your practice schedule, keep track of the time you actually spend practicing the techniques. For example, if you only spend 1/4 hour practicing your coping statements instead of the 1/2 hour you had planned, put a line through the 1/2 hour on the practice schedule and write in 1/4 hour. In this way, you can keep a record of the time you actually spend practicing the techniques. As explained earlier, the time you spend practicing the techniques will be directly related to your progress.

In addition to monitoring your time, you may want to keep a journal of your feelings. It's a wonderful way to keep track of your progress. Begin by recording how you feel about public speaking the first day you read this book. Then record your feelings after each practice session and any opportunity you have to speak in class or on the job. Be sure to record the dates. After a few months, you will be pleasantly surprised at how much your feelings and attitudes have changed.

If you find yourself not keeping your practice schedule, ask yourself these questions:

1. What am I doing that seems more important than conquering my fear of public speaking?
2. Is this alternate activity actually more important than overcoming my fear of public speaking?
3. Can I schedule my life so I can practice the techniques and still fulfill all my commitments to other people and activities?
4. What can I cut from my schedule so I can fit the practice sessions into it?

Remember, the person who is going to help you overcome speechfright the most is *you.* The best time to take responsibility to achieve your goals is *now.* If you take the time to practice these techniques and overcome your speechfright, it will be one of the best things you have ever done. So commit yourself to a practice schedule. You can do it!

12.4 PARTICIPATE IN PUBLIC COMMUNICATION

The final step you need to take is to participate in public communication so you can put your new knowledge, techniques, and skills to use. If you are not enrolled in a public speaking course or business and professional speaking class or workshop, you need to enroll in one soon. As covered in Chapter Ten, skills training is one of the important techniques to learn in conquering speechfright. In a public speaking class you will be given many opportunities to learn, practice, and improve your new speaking skills.

Many universities offer classes or workshops for students who experience public speaking anxiety. These classes often include help in learning the fear-reduction techniques covered in this handbook and training in public speaking skills, along with numerous opportunities to practice public communication in a supportive environment.

If your local university or community college does not offer a special communication class for those who experience excessive anxiety about public communication, sign up for a public speaking fundamentals class anyway. As soon as you enroll, tell your instructor that you are working on a goal to overcome speechfright. Ask for any suggestions the instructor can give you. Show your instructor this handbook. Continue to work with the techniques presented here. Take advantage of every opportunity to speak. Beginning public speaking classes are truly workshops where many students come with little or no experience and are able to practice in a supportive atmosphere. Also, most beginning public speaking classes will include a number of students who are apprehensive about public speaking, so you won't be alone. Remember, up to 75 percent of people report a fear or anxiety about public speaking. You might find that you will be able to help and support others.

Once you have learned public speaking skills and the techniques to conquer your fear, use them. The old adage is true, "what you don't use, you lose." The best way to stay confident and develop more skills is to use what you have. Take advantage of opportunities to speak in a classroom or on the job. Participate in a speaking club at work or join a community organization, such as Toastmasters International, that will help you use and develop effective speaking skills.

You now have the tools at hand to conquer your fear of public speaking. If you develop an action plan following the suggestions in this book, you will become a confident speaker. It will be one of the best things you have ever done. Speechfright will become a thing of your past, and many wonderful opportunities will be on your horizon.

CHAPTER SUMMARY

You can conquer your speechfright, but you must develop an action plan. You will need to 1) commit yourself to your goal, 2) actively learn the techniques, 3) practice the techniques following a schedule, and 4) participate in public communication.

The person who is going to help you conquer speechfright the most is *you*. The best time to take responsibility to achieve your goals is *now*. If you take the time to follow an action plan to conquer your speechfright, it will be one of the best things you have ever done.

REVIEW QUESTIONS

After reading this chapter, you should be able to answer the following questions:

1. Explain the four measures for developing an action plan to overcome speechfright.
2. What does active learning mean in reference to overcoming speechfright?
3. Is there a miracle cure to speechfright? How long will it take to see results?
4. What is the best way to begin participating in public communication?

REFERENCES

Allen, M., Hunter, J., & Donohue, W. (1989). Meta-analysis of self-report data on the effectiveness of public speaking anxiety treatment techniques. *Communication Education*, *38*, 54–76.

Anthony, W. P., Maddox, E. N., & Wheatley, W. (1988). *Envisionary management*. New York: Quorum Books.

Assagioli, R. (1973). *The act of will.* New York: Viking Press.

Assagioli, R. (1976). *Psychosynthesis: A manual of principles and techniques.* New York: Penguin Books.

Ayres, J. (1986). Perceptions of speaking ability: An explanation of stage fright. *Communication Education*, *35*, 275–287.

Ayres, J. (1988). Antecedents of communication apprehension: A reaffirmation. *Communication Research Reports*, *5*, 58–63.

Ayers, J. (1994). *Effective Public Speaking*. Madison, WI: WCB Brown & Benchmark.

Ayers, J., & Hopf, T. S. (1985). Visualization: A means of reducing speech anxiety. *Communication Education, 35,* 318–323.

Ayers, J., & Hopf, T. S. (1989). Is it more than extra-attention? *Communication Education, 38,* 1–5.

Ayers, J., & Hopf, T. S. (1991). Coping with writing apprehension. *Journal of Applied Communication Research, 19,* 318–323.

Ayers, J., & Hopf, T. S. (1993). *Coping with speech anxiety.* Norwood, NJ: Ablex.

Bandura, A. (1973). *Social learning theory.* Englewood Cliffs, NJ: Prentice Hall.

Beck, A. T., Rush, A. J., Shaw, B. F., & Emery, G. (1979). *Cognitive therapy of depression*. New York: Guilford.

Behnke, R. R., & Beatty, L. W. (1981). A cognitive-physiological model of speech anxiety. *Communication Monographs*, *48*, 158–163.

Benson, H. (1975). *The relaxation response.* New York: William Morrow and Company.

Booth-Butterfield, M., & Booth-Butterfield, S. (1992). *Communication apprehension and avoidance in the classroom.* Edina, MN: Burgess Publishing.

Bourne, E. J. (1990). *The anxiety & phobia workbook.* Oakland, CA: New Harbinger Publications.

Bruskin Report (1973, July). *What are Americans afraid of?* (Research Rep. No. 53).

Brydon, S., & Scott, M. (1994). *Between one and many.* Mountainview, CA: Mayfield Publishing.

Burns, D. (1980). *Feeling good: The new mood therapy.* New York: William Morrow.

Cannon, W. B. (1914). The emergency function of the adrenal medulla in pain and the major emotions. *American Journal of Physiology*, *33*, 356–372.

Carr, J. T. (1996). *Communication apprehension and exercise adherence: An exploratory study*. Unpublished master's thesis, University of Nebraska at Omaha, Omaha, NE.

Clevenger, T., & King, T. R. (1961). A factor analysis of the visible symptoms of stage fright. *Speech Monographs, 28,* 296–298.

Daly, J. A., & Buss A. H. (1984). The transitory causes of audience anxiety. In J. A. Daly and J. C. McCroskey (Eds.), *Avoiding communication*. Beverly Hills, CA: Sage.

Daly, J. G., & Stafford, L. (1984). Implications of quietness: Some facts and speculations. In J. A. Daly and J. C. McCroskey (Eds.), *Avoiding communication*. Beverly Hills, CA: Sage.

Daniels, K., & Guppy, A. (1994). Occupational stress, social support, job control, and psychological well-being. *Human Relations*, *47*, 1523–1544.

Davis, M., Eshelman, E., & McKay, M. (1988). *The relaxation and stress workbook.* Oakland, CA: New Harbinger Publications.

Desburg, P., & Marsh, G. (1988). *Controlling stagefright: Presenting yourself to audiences from one to one thousand.* Oakland, CA: New Harbinger Publications.

Dryden, W., & DiGiuseppe, R. (1990). *A primer on rational-emotive therapy*. Champaign, IL: Research Press.

Dwyer, K. (1995a). Creating and teaching special sections of a public speaking course for apprehensive students: A multi-case study. *Basic Communication Course Annual*, *7*, 100–124.

Dwyer, K. (1995b, November). *Teaching students to self-manage communication apprehension*

Harcourt Brace & Company

using the multimodal approach for self-selecting treatments. Paper presented at the Speech Communication Association Annual Meeting, San Antonio.

Ellis, A. (1962). *Reason and emotion in psychotherapy.* New York: Stuart.

Ellis, A., & Dryden, W. (1987). *The practice of rational emotive therapy.* New York: Springer Publishing.

Ellis, A., & Harper, R. E. (1975). *A new guide to rational living.* North Hollywood, CA: Wilshire Book.

Fanning, P. (1988). *Visualization for change.* Oakland, CA: New Harbinger Publications.

Fawcett, S. B., & Miller, L. K. (1975). Training public speaking behavior: An experimental analysis and social validation. *Journal of Applied Behavior Analysis, 8,* 125–135.

Fremouw, W. J., & Zitter, R. E. (1978). A comparison of skills training and cognitive restructuring-relaxation for the treatment of speech anxiety. *Behavior Therapy, 9,* 248–259.

Friedrich, G. & Goss, B. (1984). Systematic desensitization. In J. A. Daly and J. C. McCroskey (Eds.), *Avoiding communication.* Beverly Hills, CA: Sage.

Garfield, C. (1984). *Peak performance.* Los Angeles: Jeremy P. Tarcher, Inc.

Garfield, C. (1986). *Peak performers.* New York: William Morrow & Co., Inc.

Gilkerson, H. (1942). Social fears as reported by students in college speech classes. *Speech Monographs, 9,* 141–160.

Glaser, S. R. (1981). Oral communication apprehension and avoidance: The current status of treatment research. *Communication Education, 30,* 321–341.

Jacobs, E. E., Harvill, R. L., & Masson, R. L. (1988). *Group counseling strategies and skills.* Pacific Grove, CA: Brooks/Cole Publishing Company.

Jacobson, E. (1938). *Progressive relaxation.* Chicago: Chicago University Press.

Kagan, J., & Reznick, J. (1986). Shyness and temperament. In W. Jones, J. Cheek, & S. Briggs (Eds.), *Shyness: Perspectives on research and treatment* (pp. 81–90). New York: Plenum Press.

Kagan, J., Reznick, J., & Snidman, N. (1988). Biological bases of childhood shyness. *Science, 240,* 167–171.

Kelly, L. (1989). Implementing a skills training program for reticent communicators. *Communication Education, 38,* 85–101.

Kelly, L., Duran, R., & Stewart, J. (1990). Rhetoritherapy revisited: A test of its effectiveness as a treatment for communication problems. *Communication Education, 39,* 207–266.

Lazarus, A. (1989). *The practice of multimodal therapy.* Baltimore, MD: John Hopkins University Press.

Manchester, W. (1967). *The death of a president, November 20–November 25.* New York: Harper & Row.

McCroskey, J. C. (1972). The implementation of a large-scale program of systematic desensitization for communication apprehension. *Speech Teacher, 21,* 255–264.

McCroskey, J. C. (1977). Oral communication apprehension: A review of recent theory and research. *Human Communication Research, 4,* 78–96.

McCroskey, J. C. (1982). Oral communication apprehension: A reconceptualization. In M. Burgoon (Ed.), *Communication yearbook 6.* Beverly Hills, CA: Sage.

McCroskey, J. C. (1984). The communication apprehension perspective. In J. A. Daly and J. C. McCroskey (Eds.), *Avoiding communication.* Beverly Hills, CA: Sage.

McCroskey, J. C. (1993). *An introduction to rhetorical communication* (6th ed.). Englewood Cliffs, NJ: Prentice Hall.

McCroskey, J. C., Ralph, D. C., & Barrick, J. E. (1970). The effect of systematic desensitization on speech anxiety. *Speech Teacher, 19,* 32–36.

Meichenbaum, D. (1977). *Cognitive-behavior modification.* New York: Plenum.

Motley, M. (1990). Public speaking anxiety qua performance anxiety: A revised model and an alternative therapy. *Journal of Social Behavior and Personality, 5,* 85–104.

Motley, M. (1991). Public speaking anxiety qua performance anxiety: A revised model and an alternative therapy. In M. Booth-Butterfield (Ed.) *Communication, cognition, and anxiety.* Newbury Park, CA: Sage.

Motley, M. (1995). *Overcoming your fear of public speaking—A proven method*. New York: McGraw-Hill.

Motley, M., & Molloy, J. (1994). An efficacy test of a new therapy ("Communication-Orientation Motivation") for public speaking anxiety. *Journal of Social Behavior and Personality*, *22*, 48–58.

O'Keefe, E. (1985). Multimodal self-management: A holistic approach to teaching self-improvement. *Human Education and Development*, *6,* 176–181.

Otto, J. (1990). The effects of physical exercise on psychophysiological reactions under stress. *Cognition and Emotion*, *4*, 341–357.

Overholser, J. C., Norman, W. H., & Miller, I. W. (1990). Life stress and social support in depressed patients. *Behavioral Medicine*, *4,* 125–131.

Paul, G. (1966). *Insight vs. desensitization in psychotherapy.* Palo Alto, CA: Stanford University Press.

Phillips, G. M. (1977). Rhetoritherapy versus the medical model: Dealing with reticence. *Communication Education, 26,* 34–43.

Phillips, G. M. (1991). *Communication incompetencies*. Carbondale, IL: Southern Illinois University Press.

Pucel J., & Stocker, G. (1983). A nonverbal approach to communication: A cross-cultural study of stress behaviors. *Communication, 12,* 53–65.

Ray, E. B., & Miller, K. I. (1994). Social support, home/work stress, and burnout: Who can help? *Journal of Applied Behavioral Science, 30*, 357–373.

Richmond, V., & McCroskey, J. C. (1995). *Communication: Apprehension, avoidance, and effectiveness* (4th ed.). Scottsdale, AZ: Gorsuch Scarisbrick.

Rice, P. L. (1987). *Stress and Health*. Pacific Grove, CA: Brooks/Cole Publishing Company.

Rossi, A. M., & Seiler, W. J. (1989). The comparative effectiveness of systematic desensitization and an integrative approach to treating public speaking anxiety. *Imagination, Cognition, and Personality*, *9*, 49–66.

Sachs, M. L. (1982). Exercise and running: Effects on anxiety, depression, and psychology. *Humanistic Education and Development*, *21*, 51–57.

Schwartz, S. G., & Kloupek, D. G. (1987). Acute exercise combines with imaginal exposure as a technique for anxiety reduction. *Canadian Journal of Behavioral Science*, *19*, 151–166.

Sedlock, D., & Duda, J. (1994). The effect of trait anxiety and fitness level on heart rate and state anxiety responses to mental arithmetic stressor among college-age women. *International Journal of Sports Psychology*, *25*, 218–229.

Seligmann, J., & Peyser, M. (1994). Drowning on dry land. *Newsweek*, *123*, 64–66.

Simpson, B. A. (1982). *The role of perceived self-efficacy in three treatments of speech anxiety.* Dissertation Abstracts International, *42*, *4590-B*. (University Microfilms No. 8209222.)

Stone, W. J. (1987). *Adult fitness programs: Planning, designing, managing, and improving fitness programs*. Glenview, IL: Scott Foresman.

U. S. Department of Health and Human Services. (1991). *Healthy people 2000: National health promotion and disease prevention objectives.* (DDHS Publication No.1 PHS 91-50212) Washington, D.C.: U.S. Government Printing Office.

Van Kleeck, A., & Daly, J. A. (1982). Instructional communication research and theory: Communication development and instructional communication—A review. In M. Burgoon (Ed.), *Communication Yearbook*, *5.* New Brunswick, NJ: Transaction Books.

Wallechinsky, D., Wallace, I., & Wallace, A (1977). *The book of lists.* New York: Bantam Books.

Watts, F. (1979). *Habituation model of systematic desensitization. Psychological Bulletin, 86,* 627–637.

Whitworth, R. H., & Cochran, C. (1996). Evaluation of integrated versus unitary treatments for reducing public speaking anxiety. *Communication Education*, *45*, 306–314.

Wolpe, J. (1958). *Psychotherapy by reciprocal inhibition*. Palo Alto, CA: Stanford University Press.

Yates, A. (1975). *Theory and practice in behavior therapy*. New York: John Wiley.

SUBJECT INDEX

Order Your copy of <u>Conquering Speechfright</u> Audio Tape!

Wipe out your speechfright with this unique, one-of-a-kind audio tape—exclusively prepared by the author of this text! This 100-minute cassette takes you through the cognitive restructuring process helping you isolate your worrisome and fearful thoughts about public speaking. The audio tape gives you ways to change your negative thoughts into productive coping thoughts and helps you learn relaxation techniques.

For only $6.95*, *Conquering Speechfright* will teach you to:

- Learn positive coping statements to replace your negative thoughts
- Learn systematic desensitization (deep muscle relaxation and positive mental imagery)
- Learn the mental rehearsal technique to prepare you for a successful presentation
- Learn effective deep abdominal breathing exercises to reduce pre-speech anxiety.

Order your copy of *Conquering Speechfright* directly from Harcourt Brace. Please complete this order form and mail it to the address listed below or call 1-800-782-4479.

Indicate Credit Card ( ) AMEX ( ) MasterCard ( ) VISA

Credit card number ______________________________

Name as shown on card______________________________

Expiration date ______________________________

Your signature______________________________

Name ______________________________

Address ______________________________

City ______________________ State_______ Zip code ____________

Phone number ( )______________________

Please mail this form to: Harcourt Brace College Publishers
Reference Number
Order Fulfillment Department
6277 Sea Harbor Drive
Orlando, FL 32887

*Plus Shipping (allow 3–4 weeks for delivery)

Harcourt Brace & Company